MW00636346

Crested Butte Colorado

60 Scenic Day Hikes

by Anne and Mike Poe

www.hikingbikingadventures.com

Cover photo by Mike Poe
View of Snowmass Mountain from Hasley Pass

Crested Butte Colorado

60 Scenic Day Hikes

by Anne and Mike Poe

www. hikingbikingadventures.com

Editing
Michael Bragg

Cover Design and Book Layout
Sheryl Evans
Evans Studios
www.Evans-Studios.com

Photography
Anne and Mike Poe

Layout Design and Map Composition
Rebecca Finkel
F&P Graphic Design
www.fpgd.com

ISBN 978-0-9829766-0-9

Printed in China by Everbest Printing Co. through Four Colour Print Group

Dedication

To the Alpha-1 community.
May we all continue to live life to our fullest capacity.

Acknowledgements

Writing a book is never the effort of a single person. My gratitude belongs first to my husband, Mike, who has supported, encouraged, believed in, and accompanied me throughout this journey physically and emotionally. From contributing trail descriptions and great photographs to total content review, his involvement created a shared effort. This publication would never have seen fruition without his full participation.

Our gratitude extends especially to Dick Baroni. His analytical talents have been instrumental to developing a system for difficulty ratings that use a mathematical approach to a very subjective process. His attention to detail and willingness to review the descriptions has helped us to view the explanations from an avid hikers' perspective.

Charles Wells, established author and publisher of 4-wheel drive adventure guide books, (FunTreks.com), gave freely of his time and experience. He shared his extensive knowledge of the technical side of publishing, and answered our endless questions with gracious patience. Through his help, we gained necessary information, and a new friend. Thank you, Chuck.

Our thanks as well go to Jean King, who patiently worked through the descriptions to test their clarity and clear up confusions. We thank her for her infectious enthusiasm. All projects need cheerleaders to encourage lofty goals, and keep spirits running high. To Gene King, the other half of the family whose internet knowledge has shown us marketing opportunities we would never have understood on our own. Thank you good friends for your endless support.

To Rebecca Finkel, layout designer, who with patience extra-ordinary worked with a myriad of maps, text, and photos, artfully weaving them into the tapestry that became this book.

I extend my earnest gratitude to Michael Bragg, who edited the entire content of this work for grammatical errors, consistency in presentation, and data accuracy. His research and keen eye for detail corrected many a flaw that numerous reviews on my part would not have recognized.

To Sheryl Evans, Evans Studios, www.evans-studios.com, who with a wealth of talent, took the design and layout of the printed book to completion, and produced the e-book, download version. She designed, and brought to life our web site, www.hikingbikingadventures.com, converted our other publications into e-format, and showed me how to be the master of my own computer. Thank you for your efficiency, and always positive outlook.

Printing a first book is a scary proposition. Printing a full color book requires careful and precise skill. There is too much for a novice to learn. Thanks to Chris Carpenter of Four Colour Print Group who with expert advice guided us through the hoops of quality color printing and proofing.

We extend special thanks to all you hikers we met on the trail. Your enthusiasm for this book has spurred us on. Your ideas about what kind of information you would like to see in a hiking guide helped shape the content and format of this book. You asked for a scenic rating system, a difficulty rating system that included important facts on elevation, topographical maps in color with easy to read information printed directly on them, and lots of color photography showing the scenic value of the hike. Many of you are featured in these photos, hiking the trails where we met.

Introduction

Why this Guidebook is Different

This book is exclusively day hikes, written for you, the day hiker. You love to hike, but you don't have any interest in shuttling a heavy pack on your back, or sleeping on the ground. You prefer to hike light and return to your camper or hotel for a good meal and a comfortable sleep. All the hikes in this book can be walked in a day. There are long ones, short ones, easy ones, and difficult ones, but after each hike you can sleep in a bed.

As avid day hikers ourselves, we have found over the years that our time has become more precious. When we go to a new area, it takes effort to research what hikes are right for us. Often, we are visiting the area for just a weekend, or a week, and wish to find the best hike we can for the time we have. We are very particular about the kind of hikes we are looking for. We have also discovered, in conversation with many day hikers we met along the trail, that they too have specific parameters in mind when selecting a hike. Our values are incredibly similar.

Scarp Ridge

When we hike, we want to be wowed. We want to be thrilled along the way with views of looming peaks and cascading rivers plunging into profound chasms. We like vistas that stretch from horizon to horizon. We like precipitous cliffs and trails that cling to them. We like to descend into massive river canyons. We like intriguing twists and turns that hide, then reveal their secrets as we round each corner. We want to surround ourselves with fields of bright and cheery wildflowers spilling across acres of colorful meadows, the horizon exploding with peaks and valleys demanding exploration. We like color: wildflowers, aspens, oak, red rocks, turquoise lakes, big skies. We want killer photo opportunities.

We don't like to hike for miles in thick, viewless forests. We are not fond of scrub and brush that stands taller than our five foot, five inch frames. We are quickly irritated by cantankerous boulder strewn trails that force our eyes downward. We dislike hiking an uninspired trail all day for the sake of one final viewpoint.

When we go purposely to a wilderness area to hike, we are looking for more than just exercise. We want the remaining wilderness pieces of our world to awaken our primordial senses and unleash our civilized constraints. We want to feel the pulse of wild nature course through our veins as it energizes and quickens our step. We want to be overwhelmed by so much splendor that it spills over in enthusiasm for days thereafter. We seek the superlatives Mother Nature created.

Many hiking guides leave us guessing as to what the trail really has to offer. How many times have you read a trail description that tells you where to start and end, but offers no clues as to what might excite you along the way? How do you really know if you want to spend your precious time on this hike? Like us, many hikers are engaged in the art of guessing when it comes to choosing a satisfactory trail.

A guidebook should guide. Its purpose is to provide a variety of information and detail so the reader can decide which hikes are personally most suitable. In addition to important information such as distance, difficulty, and other basics, we think there should be a rating system for scenic value. Of course, like difficulty ratings, scenic ratings are subjective. This system developed around our personal preferences, and from around preferences other hikers have shared with us. We have personally hiked every trail in this book. We have rated these hikes using criteria that is essential to us when choosing to do a particular hike. We hope our system helps you find the trails that are worth your precious time.

Scenic Rating System

Six Stars: These are often hikes that go up peaks or to high passes where expansive vistas evoke the feeling of Rocky Mountain grandeur. To qualify for 6 stars, however, the journey along the trail must be equally stimulating. The entire hiking time is inspiring, with many different vistas to contemplate.

Five Stars: You may not ascend a peak or hike to a pass. The scenic splendor of the trail may be manifested in following a rushing stream, or winding through a grove of stately aspens. Dramatic vistas are frequent, becoming consistent. There are beaver ponds, lakes, wildflowers, expansive meadows, peaks, gorges. Many views encompass a staggering 180 degrees. You will want to hike this trail again and again.

Four Stars: The scenery is grand along the way, but it is less consistent. There are some short sections hiking through dense forest. The high adrenaline experience is not as sustained as a six or five star hike, but the experience is exhilarating, and you will look forward to repeating this hike.

Three Stars: These hikes are very worthwhile, as there are numerous vistas along the way. More time may be spent hiking through forests, but the forests are mature and healthy and create an overall feeling of beauty and tranquility. It is a very satisfying hike.

Two Stars: These trails, for much of the total distance, pass through thick forest with only occasional views. The destination would be rated much higher if it were not for the less interesting approach. Hikers can decide if the destination is worth the effort.

One Star: These hikes travel mostly through forest that may have more deadfall. The trees are not as stately. There are fewer vistas. The area feels overused. The destination is not really special compared to other choices.

Highlights Section

In addition to the star ratings, there is a highlights box near the beginning of every hike. This is your instant reference to what you will see on this hike. You do not need to read the Trail Description to know if you want to do this hike.

Why Day Hiking is so Good around Crested Butte

Crested Butte lies in the stunning, wildflower-covered meadowland of the East River Valley, surrounded by the Gunnison National Forest. Five Wilderness areas are carved from this forest. The hikes in this book penetrate three of these, and they are easily accessible from Crested Butte.

Perhaps the least visited is the West Elk Wilderness, which spreads out to the southwest of Crested Butte. Fortified by the West Elk Mountains, Storm Ridge, the Castles, and the Anthracite Range, this wilderness combines expansive wildflower meadows and aspen forests, which flow between the monumental ranges. Part of the largest contiguous aspen forest in the United States resides in this wilderness.

The Ragged Wilderness, just ten miles northwest of Crested Butte, is where the rest of that contiguous aspen forest flourishes. These stately trees smother the hillsides and valleys in glorious gold and orange every fall while Gambrel oak adds startling red to the scene. The rugged, sharp peaks of the Ruby Range, stand-alone Marcellina Mountain, and the distant Elk Range tower above the colorful benchland, while Anthracite Creek carves the mysterious 500-foot deep Dark Canyon below. Adding to the astounding geological variety of this wilderness area is the glacier-carved alpine tundra of Oh Be Joyful Basin.

Due north of Crested Butte, the massive 14,000-foot peaks of the Maroon Bells-Snowmass Wilderness area in the White River National Forest stand guard. Between Crested Butte and Aspen, six of Colorado's famous fourteeners dominate this wilderness—a formidable barrier. You will see more hikers on these trails, as the wildflowers backed by dramatic peaks are a major draw.

Each of the five valleys radiating out from Crested Butte gives access to these wilderness areas and their superlative hikes. Each valley displays its own variety of flowers, trees, canyons, peaks, and meadows that makes it unique. Each valley also offers trails that differ in character, feeling, distance, and difficulty from those found in the others. These valleys, along with maps showing the trailhead for each hike and campsites nearby, are described in the hiking section of the book.

Crested Butte functions as the hub of this hiking heaven. There are enough trails of exquisite variety in the Crested Butte area to thrill day hikers for many years. The premier quality of these hikes form the reason for writing this guidebook.

Best Season to Hike

Winter is cold and snows stay long in the mountains around Crested Butte. Generally, the earliest a hiker can trek this high country is late June or early July, depending on winter's accumulation of snowfall. Snows return in short storms by the first week in October in these mountains. Short as the season may be, it is blessed with incredible highlights. Starting mid-July, wildflowers cover the high mountain meadows in full splendor. They flourish into early and sometimes mid-August. Then the aspens unveil their glory. By mid-September, the golden color is creeping into the canopy. It spreads day by day until that first week in October when snows signal the inevitable coming of winter.

Short Loop to Frigid Air Pass

How to Use this Guide

Find the Hikes You Want

The table of contents is innovative. It is a complete chart that, at a glance, provides you with information to help you search for a particular hike: star rating, difficulty level, distance, shuttle, loop, or out & back hike, popular bike and horse trails, the best wildflower and aspen hikes, and vehicle access.

To further aid in your search for the perfect hike, the book is divided into six chapters, one for each valley and the trailheads located there. Each chapter begins with an introduction to the valley, how many trails are accessed from it, and a little about their character. There you will find the topographical map of the valley, with the trailheads numbered. Additional maps and charts in Appendix 1 detail many of the dispersed campsites in each valley.

Difficulty

Like scenic ratings, difficulty is subjective. We use six categories to help you define for yourself how difficult the hike would be for you: distance, difficulty rating, surface, gradient, highest elevation, and elevation gain and/or loss.

DISTANCE is expressed as the total mileage it takes to complete the out & back, the loop, or to arrive at the shuttle point.

DIFFICULTY RATING is a summary assessment of the total hike that takes into consideration distance, surface conditions, gradient, highest elevation, and elevation gain or loss. The categories are as follows: easy, easy to moderate, moderate, moderate to difficult, difficult, very difficult.

SURFACE: Are you walking on packed dirt or stumbling over and around rocks and roots? Is the trail slick, is there loose talus that requires extra caution, or can you watch the scenery go by? Since no trail has the same surface conditions from start to finish, we have written a brief description of the various conditions encountered.

GRADIENT affects most hikers more than distance. We divide gradient into the following categories: easy, moderate, steep, and very steep.

- **Easy Gradient:** Trail climbs between 0 to 400 feet per mile.
- **Moderate gradient:** Trail climbs between 400 to 800 feet per mile.
- **Steep gradient:** Trail climbs between 800 to 1,000 feet per mile.
- **Very steep gradient:** Trail climbs over 1,000 feet per mile.

If "sustained" is used, it indicates there are no breaks in this stretch for a long way!

HIGHEST ELEVATION: All the hikes in this book start above 9,000 feet. If you come from lower elevations and wish to hike for a few days, most likely you will not be acclimatized. Researchers suggest that one adjust to higher elevations by sleeping at least one night at 8,000 feet or two nights at 7,000 feet before the hike. If you know elevation affects you, you might consider starting with easier hikes while you acclimate.

ELEVATION GAIN OR LOSS: These figures account for all the ups and downs in the trail that you have to negotiate.

Hiking Times

Assessing hiking times is even more personal than difficulty ratings. Some folks have long strides, others like to keep a slower pace. On average, we hike 2.0 mph on easy hikes, 1.5 mph on moderate, and 1.0 on difficult. We don't stop for lunch or rests other than a quick snack or a photo opportunity. Times stated are for the complete hike. We were in our late 60s at the time we hiked these trails.

Vehicle Access to Trailheads

All of the roads leading from Crested Butte up to the valleys are dirt and gravel roads. Each road is graded infrequently. Conditions vary by amount of usage and weather. Rough washboard, drainage ditches cutting across the roadbed, loose rock, very steep sections, and one lane roads with few pullovers are the major considerations. The Table of Contents lists the preferred vehicle.

- **Car** designates that any low clearance vehicle can drive the road.
- **SUV** designates that any high clearance vehicle or pick-up truck, short or long wheel base, can negotiate the road. Cars may scrape the under carriage.
- **4x4** designates that only a short wheel base, 4-wheel drive vehicle, ATV, or motorcycle can negotiate the access road.

In summary, an SUV or pickup truck can access every trailhead in this book.

We drove our Dually, 350HD extended cab pickup for every hike. Though it is a big vehicle for narrow sections, we arrived safely. We only had to use 4-wheel drive once, after a heavy rain when the road became very slick.

Map Legend
TRAIL COLORS:

- **Green:** represents a trail section that is easy or easy to moderate.
- **Blue:** represents moderate and moderate to difficult.
- **Red :** represents difficult and very difficult.
- The featured trail is shown in green, blue, red, or a combination of colors to designate where the trail changes from one difficulty level to another.
- **Purple:** represents connecting trails not discussed in the book.

OTHER MARKERS:

- **GPS Waypoints:** Numbers highlighted by a colored circle on the maps and in the text.
- **Elevations:** given for each GPS point on the map where space permits.
- **Mileage:** given for each GPS point from the start of the hike—where space permits.
- **Green Tent:** is for Forest Service campground.
- **Black Tent:** is for free dispersed, undeveloped camping areas.
- **P symbol:** represents a parking area.
- **CBVC:** Crested Butte Visitor Center.
- **Junction:** We use the word "junction" on the maps, in the text, and GPS charts. We use the general definition: a place where things join. We want the word to send up a red flag when you read it: look for a connecting trail. It may be very faint. Many "junctions" are not signed. Some are signed, but may not match the maps you purchased. A lot of very exciting trails in this book follow an unsigned trail.

DOGS: are permitted on every trail.

GPS Charts

Many hikers now carry a GPS unit. It is lots of fun to know the elevation and distance as you follow a route. We use the GPS to provide you with accurate data. (See GPS data below for error factor.) Instead of long descriptions, the GPS chart puts all that data in one quick and easy reference.

The GPS number, the first column in the chart, corresponds to the number in the circle on the map. Follow the numbers in column one, and you will see the route for that hike on the map. The chart then lists the mileage covered to each point, the co-ordinates, elevation, and special considerations.

GPS Data

We obtained distance and elevation data using a Garmin E-Trex Venture HC series GPS. The E-Trex has an elevation error factor of +/- 25 feet and a distance error factor of +/- 10 feet.

Carry this Guide

There is a lot of information in this guidebook. It is meant to be carried with you when you hike. When you hike Trail 23, you will pass the routes to 6 other hikes. Since all seven hikes are on the same map, your understanding and appreciation of the area will grow exponentially. It allows you to see the terrain for a future hike or change your mind and hike a different trail on the spur of the moment. You will know where that intriguing trail goes. Other hikers may inspire you to go on their favorite trail. The information you need is in your hands.

When you carry the book, you can consult the GPS charts to know how far you have gone and how much time you may linger before turning back. You will know what to expect ahead, what is yet to see and experience.

The color coded maps give information about changing levels of difficulty along the trail. Gage your fitness and assess how far you might go.

Some of the photos have routes drawn on them to aid in finding your way. Other photos may inspire you to create your own memorable photography.

Scarp Ridge Middle Loop

Other Considerations

Weather

Weather must be considered when hiking in the Colorado Rockies. The prime high altitude hiking season is also the prime monsoon season. There are frequent afternoon thunderstorms. Be prepared for strong winds, dropping temperatures, sudden heavy rainfall, and lightning. Take warning from approaching dark clouds and plan ahead to hike down off exposed ridges. Do not take cover from lightning under lone trees, in shallow caves, or against cliff edges. If necessary, squat down and hide in brush or grass away from such objects. A safe rule of thumb is to plan arriving at your highest elevation point by noon or 1:00 P.M. at the latest so you can get to lower elevation before the thunderstorms arrive.

Water

Water is essential for hikers to maintain good condition, even more so at high elevations. Too many day hikers convince themselves they can drink when they get back because they don't want to carry the extra weight. On a cool or cloudy day, the signs of thirst are reduced, which tempts day hikers to drink even less. Don't make these mistakes. The muscles need to flush out lactic acid while you are hiking to maintain fitness.

We recommend using a bladder system as opposed to a water bottle hidden in your pack. A bladder makes it convenient to take sips every fifteen minutes whether you feel thirsty or not. For best results, drink about 16 ounces for every hour of exercise. If you are hoping to obtain water along the route from one of many streams or creeks, carry a proper filter or treat the water with iodine solution. Both products are available at most outdoor stores. Cattle and sheep, as well as wildlife, roam freely throughout this area. All water should be considered infected. On longer hikes, we also take several small bottles of water with a sports drink mixed in. It re-hydrates, replenishes, and refuels better than water alone.

High Altitude

Common signs of unhealthy reaction to elevation are headache, nausea, stumbling, and shortness of breath. There are products sold in high elevation communities to help with altitude adjustment, or you can try aspirin, but the best remedy for altitude sickness is to hike down.

Hypothermia

Hypothermia is a condition in which the internal body temperature is at least 3.6° F below the normal 98.6°. The body functions begin to slow down and deteriorate. Early symptoms are excessive shivering and slurred speech. Wearing soaked clothing in prolonged cold temperatures can precipitate the condition. Hypothermia is serious and can lead to death. Layered synthetic clothing and fleece outerwear and raingear for emergency use is prudent. Hikers should also be prepared to spend a night in the wilderness. See Prevention next page.

Prevention

Prevention is better than rescue. Regardless of the length or difficulty of hike, a prudent hiker will always follow certain rules and carry specific safety items.

- Hike with a partner, rather than alone.
- Sign in at the trailhead register if there is one. That makes it easier for rescue parties to find you.
- Tell someone where you are going and when you expect to return. Give them the license plate number of your car or the phone number of a family member or friend.
- Wear layered clothing designed to wick away sweat. Cotton is not recommended.
- Wear ankle supporting boots with good tread as opposed to sandals or sneakers.
- In addition to food and water, always carry the following items: rain gear, flashlight, basic first aid kit, matches or lighter, pocket knife, sunglasses, sunscreen, sunhat, extra clothing, map and compass, emergency shelter or space blanket, insect repellent.

Colorado Rescue Insurance

A Colorado Outdoor Recreation Search and Rescue card (CORSAR) can be purchased at all Forest Service locations and most outdoor stores throughout Colorado for $3.00 per person per year or $12.00 for 5 years. This is a bargain. If you are in trouble and the search and rescue team helps you get out to safety, there will be no charge for this service unless helicopter rescue is required. In that case, your regular health insurance would have to take over.

View from Kebler Pass Road

Table of Contents

Dedication   iii

Acknowledgements   iv

Introduction   v - vii
    Why This Guidebook Is Different   v
    Scenic Rating System   vi
    Highlights Box   vi
    Why Day Hiking is so Good around Crested Butte   vi
    Best Season to Hike   vii

How to Use this Guide   viii - x
    Find the Hikes You Want   viii
    Difficulty   viii
    Hiking Times   ix
    Vehicle Access to Trailheads   ix
    Map Legend   ix
    GPS Charts   x
    GPS Data   x
    Carry this Guide   x

Other Considerations   xi - xii
    Weather   xi
    Water   xi
    High Altitude   xi
    Hypothermia   xi
    Prevention   xii
    Colorado Rescue Insurance   xii

Appendix A: Campsites Description   241-244

Appendix B: Summer Events in Crested Butte   244

Meet the Authors   245

Table of Contents

Crested Butte, Colorado

Hike	Name	Stars	Difficulty	Miles	Shuttle	Loop	Out & Back	Bicycles	Horses	Flowers	Aspens	Vehicles	Page
Hikes Near Town - pg1													
1	Ski Area Summit	5		2.0			Y					Car	5
2	Upper Loop to Tony's Trail	3		2.82	Y			Y		Y	Y	Car	9
3	Upper Loop to Upper Upper Loop	1		3.95	Y			Y	Y	Y	Y	Car	11
4	Whetstone Vista to Upper Upper Loop	1		1.99		Y		Y	Y	Y	Y	Car	15
5	Lower Loop	3		7.16	Y		Y	Y	Y			Car	17
6	Green Lake	2		8.44			Y	Y				Car	20
Gothic Valley Hikes - pg23													
7	Deer Creek to Brush Creek	4		8.23	Y		Y	Y	Y	Y	Y	SUV	27
8	Judd Falls	1		1			Y					Car	33
9	Copper Creek	2		10.4			Y		Y		Y	SUV	35
10	Rustler Gulch	5		7.0			Y		Y	Y	Y	SUV	41
11	Dorothy Peak	6		6.48			Y			Y	Y	SUV	45
12	Trail 401: Rustler Gulch to Copper Creek TH.	4		3.17	Y			Y	Y	Y	Y	SUV	49
13	Trail 401: Schofield Pass to Viewpoint	5		2.66			Y	Y	Y	Y		SUV	55
14	Trail 401: Schofield Pass to West Maroon	5		3.64	Y					Y	Y	SUV	57
15	Trail 401: Schofield Pass to Mount Bellview	6		5.56			Y			Y		SUV	60
16	Trail 401: Schofield Pass to Rustler Gulch	5		5.17	Y			Y	Y	Y	Y	SUV	63
17	West Maroon to Hasley Pass Loop	6		5.50		Y				Y	Y	SUV	69
18	West Maroon to Crystal	6		6.70	Y		Y		Y			SUV	73
19	West Maroon to Frigid Air Pass	6		9.28			Y		Y	Y		SUV	76
20	West Maroon Short Loop	6		9.43		Y			Y	Y		SUV	79
21	West Maroon Long Loop	6		14.20		Y			Y	Y	Y	SUV	83
22	West Maroon to West Maroon Pass	6		7.82			Y		Y	Y		SUV	87
23	West Maroon to Aspen	5		10.22	Y				Y	Y		SUV	91
24	Paradise Pass to Yule Pass	5		4.20			Y					SUV	97
25	Paradise Pass to Yule lake	6		8.20			Y					SUV	101
26	Paradise Pass to Marble	5		7.78	Y							SUV	105
	To Beaver Ponds	5		7.12			Y					SUV	105
27	Paradise Pass to Cinnamon Mountain	6		2.0			Y					SUV	109
Washington Gulch Hikes - pg113													
28	Snodgrass Trail	3		3.53	Y			Y	Y	Y	Y	Car	117
29	Washington Gulch to Viewpoint	6		2.66			Y	Y	Y	Y		Car	120
30	Washington Gulch to Gothic	3		4.0	Y			Y	Y	Y		Car	123
31	Washington Gulch No Name Trail	4		1.0			Y					Car	126
32	Baldy Ridge	5		1.7			Y				Y	SUV	128
33	Mount Baldy	6		3.76			Y					SUV	131

Slate River Valley Hikes - pg135

Hike	Name	Stars	Difficulty	Miles	Shuttle	Loop	Out & Back	Bicycles	Horses	Flowers	Aspens	Vehicles	Page
34	Oh Be Joyful to Meadows View	4		6.66			Y		Y	Y		SUV	139
35	Oh Be Joyful to Blue Lake To Garfield Peak	5 6		11 13.36			Y Y	Y Y		Y Y	Y Y	SUV SUV	141 141
36	Oh Be Joyful to Oh Be Joyful Pass	5		12.68			Y		Y	Y		SUV	145
37	Daisy Pass to Oh Be Joyful Trailhead	5		8.62	Y				Y	Y		SUV	148

Kebler Pass Hikes - pg152

Hike	Name	Stars	Difficulty	Miles	Shuttle	Loop	Out & Back	Bicycles	Horses	Flowers	Aspens	Vehicles	Page
38	Elk Creek to Copley Lake	2		3.48			Y	Y	Y			Car	155
39	Elk Creek to Mount Emmons	2		10.42			Y	Y	Y			Car	157
40	Scarp Ridge West Loop	6		6.73		Y		Y	Y	Y		SUV	161
41	Green Lake & Ruby Peak	6		6.26			Y	Y	Y	Y	Y	SUV	165
42	Scarp Ridge Middle Loop	6		4.31		Y		Y	Y			SUV	169
43	Scarp Ridge East to Mount Emmons	6		7.9			Y	Y	Y			SUV	173
44	Dyke Trail	3		4.88	Y				Y	Y	Y	Car	177
45	Horse Ranch Park to Viewpoint	5		3.36		Y			Y		Y	Car	181
46	Horse Ranch Park Loop	5		5.08		Y			Y		Y	Car	183
47	Horse Ranch Park to Ruby Anthracite	5		12.32	Y				Y		Y	Car	186
48	Horse Ranch Park to Erickson Springs	4		13.28	Y				Y		Y	Car	191
49	Ruby Anthracite to Beaver Ponds	4		4.56		Y				Y	Y	Car	195
50	Three Lakes Loop	1		2.81		Y			Y		Y	Car	201
51	Lost Lake Slough to Beckwith Pass	4		5.3			Y	Y	Y	Y	Y	Car	204
52	Cliff Creek to Beckwith Pass	5		4.56			Y	Y	Y	Y	Y	Car	207
53	Cliff Creek to Beckwith Bench Short Cliff Creek to Beckwith Bench Long	5 5		6.88 11.24			Y	Y	Y	Y	Y	Car	210 210
54	Cliff Creek to Swampy Pass	5		12.02		Y				Y	Y	Car	214
55	Cliff Creek to Ohio Creek Road	4		10.78	Y				Y	Y	Y	Car	217

Ohio Pass Hikes - pg221

Hike	Name	Stars	Difficulty	Miles	Shuttle	Loop	Out & Back	Bicycles	Horses	Flowers	Aspens	Vehicles	Page
56	Unnamed Lake	2		3.50	Y		Y		Y	Y		Car	225
57	Old Wagon Road	3		2.31	Y				Y		Y	Car	229
58	Old Railroad Grade	4		2.0			Y	Y	Y		Y	Car	233
59	Beaver Ponds	3		1.0			Y		Y	Y	Y	Car	235
60	Mill Creek	4		2.5			Y	Y			Y	Car	239

Town Hikes

The town of Crested Butte is a treasure not to be missed. Registered as a National Historic District, it has truly remained an authentic mountain town. Historians believe wandering groups of Ute Indians populated the Gunnison valley area for about 1,000 years before the first mountain men arrived in 1810. Primarily interested in furs, these few adventurers traded with the Ute.

Explorers and surveyors, such as John Gunnison, soon followed. By 1860, gold was discovered in the creeks around Crested Butte. The town was officially established in 1880. In just three years, silver and coal dominated the commerce of the approximately 30,000 people who called the area home. When other nearby mining towns died in the silver panic of 1893, Crested Butte survived. It had a smelter and two narrow gauge railroads, which made it an important supply town.

At the turn of the century, cattle ranching took hold. In 1961, the Mt. Crested Butte Ski area opened. The town has since grown

into a major ski area famous for its powder, backcountry skiing, and relaxed ambiance. Today's population of 1,635 people sprout from these legacies. It is easy to fall in love with this charming Victorian town.

Six of the hikes in this book are close to town. All but the ski area peak ascent are lower elevation hikes that can be walked earlier and later in summer than the hikes featured in the surrounding valleys.

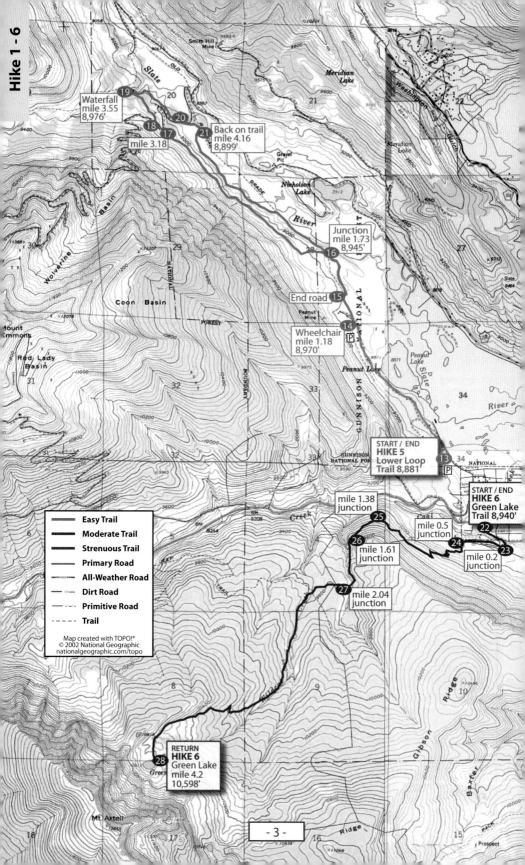

Waterfall
mile 3.55
8,976'

Back on trail
mile 4.16
8,899'

mile 3.18

Junction
mile 1.73
8,945'

End road

Wheelchair
mile 1.18
8,970'

START / END
HIKE 5
Lower Loop
Trail 8,881'

START / END
HIKE 6
Green Lake
Trail 8,940'

mile 1.38
junction

mile 0.5
junction

mile 1.61
junction

mile 0.2
junction

mile 2.04
junction

RETURN
HIKE 6
Green Lake
mile 4.2
10,598'

Easy Trail
Moderate Trail
Strenuous Trail
Primary Road
All-Weather Road
Dirt Road
Primitive Road
Trail

Map created with TOPO!®
© 2002 National Geographic
nationalgeographic.com/topo

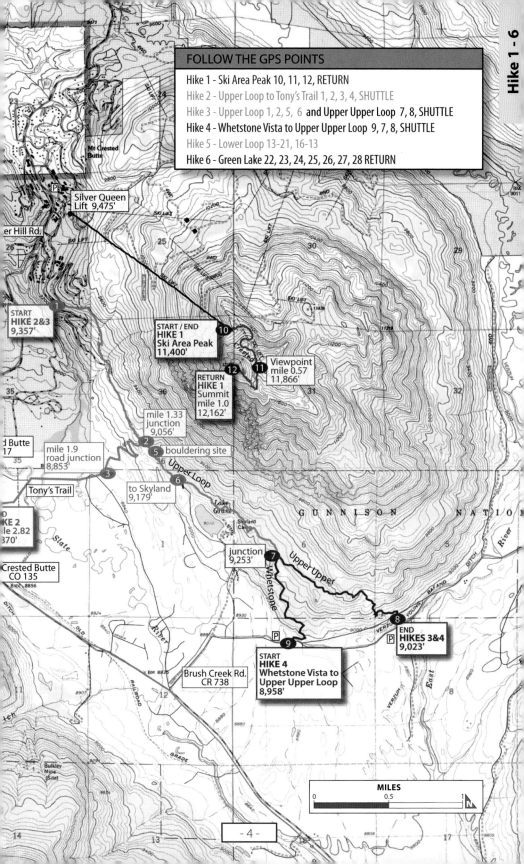

FOLLOW THE GPS POINTS

Hike 1 - Ski Area Peak 10, 11, 12, RETURN

Hike 2 - Upper Loop to Tony's Trail 1, 2, 3, 4, SHUTTLE

Hike 3 - Upper Loop 1, 2, 5, 6 **and** Upper Upper Loop 7, 8, SHUTTLE

Hike 4 - Whetstone Vista to Upper Upper Loop 9, 7, 8, SHUTTLE

Hike 5 - Lower Loop 13-21, 16-13

Hike 6 - Green Lake 22, 23, 24, 25, 26, 27, 28 RETURN

Mt Crested Butte

Silver Queen Lift 9,475'

er Hill Rd.

START HIKE 2&3 9,357'

START / END HIKE 1 Ski Area Peak 11,400'

Viewpoint mile 0.57 11,866'

RETURN HIKE 1 Summit mile 1.0 12,162'

mile 1.33 junction 9,056'

d Butte 17

mile 1.9 road junction 8,853'

bouldering site

Tony's Trail

Upper Loop

to Skyland 9,179'

KE 2 le 2.82 370'

Crested Butte CO 135

Lake Grant

Skyland Camp

GUNNISON   NATIO

junction 9,253'

Whetstone

Upper Upper

River

END HIKES 3&4 9,023'

Brush Creek Rd. CR 738

START HIKE 4 Whetstone Vista to Upper Upper Loop 8,958'

Bulkley Mine (Site)

MILES

0   0.5   1

Ski Area Summit

Distance	2.0 miles out & back.
Difficulty Rating	Very difficult.
Surface	From packed dirt steps to slippery loose rocks.
Gradient	Moderate to very steep
Average Time	2 hours
Elevations	TH: 11,400; Highest: 12,162; Gain: +888; Loss: -335 feet.
Maps	Latitude 40 Crested Butte, Taylor Park. No trail numbers.
Star Rating	

View from summit

Highlights

Take a ride on the Silver Queen lift to 11,400 feet, then hike to the summit. Here you can see the town of Crested Butte and the surrounding valleys and peaks.

Directions To Trailhead: From CBVC, drive 2.4 miles north on CR 317 to the Crested Butte Ski Area. Enter the free parking area north of the footbridge. Good signage leads you to the Silver Queen Lift. Tickets are $15 for a round trip. Opens daily from mid-June to Labor Day at 9am. Last chair down is at 2:45 pm.

Trail Description

Although the views from the summit of Crested Butte mountain are spectacular, this is not a wilderness hike. This trail starts out at a moderate gradient with high steps built into the trail. This is the easiest part. After you reach a plateau, where there are picnic tables, the trail becomes very steep, and it is difficult to ascend without some slipping. Look for Picas and Marmots in the rock slides. At the top of the second plateau, there is a short trail to a viewpoint **11**.

From this point, the trail descends steeply for 335 feet. The serious climbing begins after this descent. The trail is routed through the giant boulders that make up the flanks of the summit. Trail signs aid in keeping you on route, but halfway up the trail gets faint. Keep going up, rather than turning left or right. Be prepared for rocks moving under foot and use your hands for balance and climbing. The summit itself is a tiny perch but you will feel well protected by the surrounding rock wall. Sign your name in the book. You did it!

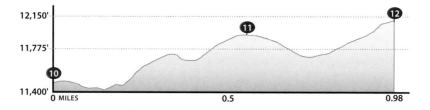

GPS	Mile	Latitude	Longitude	Elevation	Comment
10	0.0	38,53,13N	106,56,40W	11,400'	Top of Silver Queen Lift. Start hike.
11	0.57	38,53,0N	106,56,29W	11,866'	Second plateau. Viewpoint.
12	1.0	38,53,0N	106,56,37W	12,162'	Summit.

View along trail

Rocky scramble to summit

Upper Loop to Tony's Trail

View along trail

Distance	2.82 miles from start to shuttle point.
Difficulty Rating	Easy.
Surface	Easy packed dirt.
Gradient	Easy downhill.
Average Time	1 hour, 30 minutes.
Elevations	TH: 9,357; Highest: 9,357; Gain: + 137; Loss: -613
Maps	Latitude 40 Crested Butte, Taylor Park. Trails 435 to 603

Star Rating

Highlights

This is an easy trail descending gently to town. Many vistas of the Slate River Valley, the town, and the surrounding open areas. Wildflowers and aspen color in season. Good trail for early and late summer hiking.

> **Directions To Trailhead:** From CBVC, drive north 1.85 miles on Gothic Road CR 317 to Hunter Hill Road. Turn right (SE) and drive 0.8 miles to marked trailhead and parking.

> **Shuttle:** Trail ends at east end of Elk Avenue. A free shuttle bus leaves the CBVC every 20 minutes. It would drop you off at the beginning of Hunter Hill Road. Walk 0.8 miles from there to your car at the trailhead.

Trail Description

This is the easiest and most picturesque trail of the three Upper Loop trails we describe. There are more views of Crested Butte and the surrounding countryside. It is a pleasant hike, and offers a good perspective of the town and its environs.

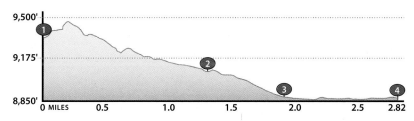

GPS	Mile	Latitude	Longitude	Elevation	Comment
1	0.0	38,53,22N	106,57,58W	9,357'	Start Upper Loop to Tony's Trail.
2	1.33	38,52,33N	106,57,21W	9,056'	Junction: Tony's Trail.
3	1.9	38,52,23N	106,57,39W	8,852'	Tony's Trail meets with county road.
4	2.82	38,52,11N	106,58,33W	8,870'	Finish hike at east end of Elk Avenue.

View approaching town

Upper Loop To
Upper Upper Loop

3

Distance	3.95 miles from start to shuttle point.
Difficulty Rating	Easy to moderate.
Surface	Alternating packed dirt and broken rock.
Gradient	Easy downhill to Lake Grant; easy uphill to mile 3.
	Steep downhill to finish.
Average Time	2 hours, 30 minutes.
Elevations	TH: 9,357; Highest: 9,357; Gain: +466; Loss: -842
Maps	Latitude 40 Crested Butte, Taylor Park. Trails 435 to 435.1
Star Rating	

Lake Grant and Skyland Subdivision

Highlights

Early and late season hiking opportunity. Summer wildflowers in season and fall aspen color are the best reasons for hiking this trail.

Directions To Trailhead: From CBVC, drive north 1.85 miles on Gothic Road CR 317 to Hunter Hill Road. Turn right (SE) and drive 0.8 miles to marked trailhead and parking.

Shuttle: From CBVC, drive 2.07 miles south on CO 135 to Brush Creek Road CR 738. Turn left (NE) and drive 1.84 miles to Upper Upper trailhead sign. Minimal parking along road.

Trail Description

This is the longer of the two hikes described for the Upper Loop trail system. It is also the more difficult of the two, although it is still a moderate hike. If you took the Whetstone Vista Trail to Brush Creek Road, there would be a little less climbing.

The more scenic part of the hike is from the start to Lake Grant junction **6**. After this junction, the trail climbs steadily through aspen and spruce forest with few vistas.

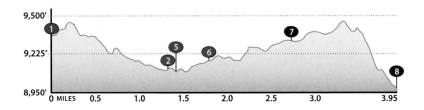

Bouldering rock

No views after Lake Grant

GPS	Mile	Latitude	Longitude	Elevation	Comment
1	0.0	38,53,22N	106,57,58W	9,357'	Start Upper Loop to Upper Upper Loop.
2	1.33	38,52,33N	106,57,21W	9,056'	Junction: to Tony's Trail.
5	1.43	38,52,30N	106,57,17W	8,948'	Junction: to bouldering site.
6	1.81	38,52,20N	106,57,2W	9,179'	Junction: to Lake Grant & Skyland.
7	2.79	38,51,53N	106,56,18W	9,253'	Junction: Upper Upper Loop and Whetstone Vista
8	3.95	38,51,32N	106,55,23W	9,023'	Finish Upper to Upper Upper Loop.
9	3.69	38,51,23N	106,56,11W	8,958'	Alternate finish: Whetstone Vista.

Whetstone Vista to

4 # Upper Upper Loop

Distance	1.99-mile loop.
Difficulty Rating	Moderate.
Surface	Alternating packed dirt and broken rock.
Gradient	Moderate uphill and downhill.
Average Time	1 hour, 30 minutes.
Elevations	TH: 8,958; Highest: 9,458; Gain: +502
Maps	Latitude 40 Crested Butte, Taylor Park. Trails 602 to 435.1
Star Rating	

Highlights

Summer wildflowers and fall aspen color are the best reasons for hiking this trail. Because of the lower elevations, it can be hiked earlier in Spring and later in Fall than many of the hikes west of Crested Butte. There are some good down valley views.

View down valley

Directions To Trailhead: From CBVC, drive 2.07 miles south on CO 135 to Brush Creek Road CR 738. Turn left (NE) and drive 1.04 miles to Whetstone Vista trailhead sign. Minimal parking along road.

Trail Description

This is a very short hike. You may meet many locals who enjoy walking from their homes to do this loop. There are good vistas down valley as you hike up and around, though much of the trail passes through dense aspen forest.

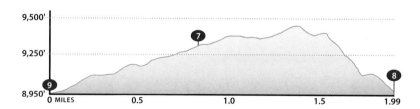

GPS	Mile	Latitude	Longitude	Elevation	Comment
9	0.0	38,51,23N	106,56,11W	8,958'	Start Whetstone Vista to Upper Upper Loop
7	0.83	38,51,53N	106,56,18W	9,253'	Junction: Upper Upper Loop.
8	1.99	38,51,32N	106,55,23W	9,023'	Finish Whetstone Vista to Upper Upper Loop. Walk west on road .80 miles back to car.

Lower Loop

Slate River Valley from trail

Distance	7.16-mile loop.
Difficulty Rating	Easy.
Surface	Easy packed dirt.
Gradient	Easy.
Average Time	3 hours, 30 minutes.
Elevations	TH: 8,881; Highest; 9,081; Gain: +370
Maps	Latitude 40 Crested Butte, Taylor Park. No trail numbers.
Star Rating	

Highlights

An easy trail with mountain views that partially follows the Slate River.

Directions To Trailhead: From CBVC, drive west on Elk Avenue. Turn right (N) on First Street. Turn left (W) on Butte Avenue, which runs into Peanut Mill road. There is a small parking area on the right. Start walking here. Wheelchair users are permitted to drive 1.18 miles more and park on the left.

Trail Description

This is one of the oldest and most popular trails in Crested Butte. A portion of the trail was used to access the mines and was also used for recreation, as it leads to beaver ponds and the Slate River. Names of some of the earlier settlers of the area are carved in the rocks on the lower loop near the beaver ponds. There are excellent views of the Slate River and Crested Butte (the mountain) along this trail. Hike this trail for any distance you desire.

This description follows the loop clockwise. The trail is well signed and easy to follow until just before Oh Be Joyful Canyon **17**. The trail meets Gunsight Pass Road. Go up Gunsight Pass Road a short distance to find the trail again **18**. There is a sign. When you come to a mining building, follow the minor road to the left of it, not the right. This will bring you to the rapids marked on the map **19**. The trail follows the river downstream for a short distance, then returns to Gunsight Pass Road **20**. (Some bikers and hikers skip this trip to the rapids by going down Gunsight Pass Road at **17** instead of up.)

After the trail joins Gunsight Pass Road again, go down the road to a lesser road that turns off to the right. Follow this secondary road a very short distance to a hiking trail that is signed **21**. Turn right (S) on this trail. Now the trail is easy to follow all the way back to your car.

Slate River and Crested Butte Mountain

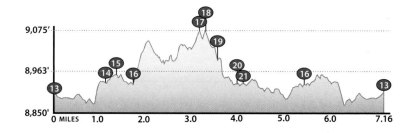

GPS	Mile	Latitude	Longitude	Elevation	Comment
13	0.0	38,52,28N	106,59,32W	8,881'	Start Lower Loop.
14	1.18	38,53,15N	107,0,17W	8,970'	Wheelchair parking.
15	1.38	38,53,25N	107,0,22W	8,965'	No cars beyond here.
16	1.73	38,53,40N	107,0,29W	8,945'	Junction: take left fork.
17	3.18	38,54,23N	107,1,44W	9,045'	Go left (W) up Gunsight Pass Road.
18	3.25	38,54,25N	107,1,48W	9.078'	Meet trail again. Turn right (NW).
19	3.55	38,54,37N	107,2,0W	8,976'	Waterfall.
20	3.96	38,54,27N	107,1,39W	8,859'	Meet Gunsight Pass Road again. Go down (E).
21	4.16	38,54,23N	107,1,28W	8,899'	Meet signed trail. Turn right (S).
16	5.43	38,53,40N	107,0,29W	8,945'	Junction: take left fork to return.
15	5.78	38,53,25N	107,0,22W	8,965'	Enter road again.
14	5.98	38,53,15N	107,0,17W	8,970'	Wheelchair parking.
13	7.16	38,52,28N	106,59,32W	8,881'	Finish Lower Loop.

Crested Butte Mountain from trail

Green Lake

Green Lake

Start of trail through subdivision

Distance	8.44 miles out & back.
Difficulty Rating	Moderate. Moderate to difficult last mile.
Surface	Easy packed dirt most of the way.
Gradient	Moderate. Almost steep for the last mile.
Average Time	5 hours.
Elevations	TH: 8,940; Highest: 10,598; Gain: +1,689
Maps	Latitude 40 Crested Butte, Taylor Park. No trail number.
Star Rating	

Highlights

Close to town hike that is popular with the locals for a quick getaway. The trail is easy on the feet, and the steady uphill gradient provides a good aerobic workout.

Directions To Trailhead: From CBVC, drive west on Elk Avenue. Turn left (S) on Second Street and go to the Nordic Center parking lot. There is no sign indicating the trailhead. Walk southeast on the gravel road on the south side of the Nordic Center, around the corner. There are trail signs from that point on.

Trail Description

We do not consider this a wilderness hike. The trail is a combination of old mining roads, new subdivision roads, and single track that pass through dense spruce forest. It is an energetic hike, with almost 1,700 feet of elevation gain in a little over 4 miles. Green Lake is interesting as a destination, but not as spectacular as other natural features in the area. There is no sign at the trailhead, but once past the first 0.2 miles all junctions between roads and trails are well marked.

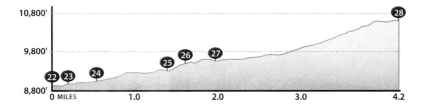

Trail follows new subdivision road

Green Lake

GPS	Mile	Latitude	Longitude	Elevation	Comment
22	0.0	38,52,2N	106,59,15W	8,940'	Start Green Lake.
23	0.20	38,51,56N	106,59,7W	8,953'	Junction: turn right (W) on road.
24	0.50	38,51,57N	106,59,26W	9,037'	Leave road and enter trail.
25	1.38	38,52,6N	107,0,5W	9,111'	Junction: old 4x4 road. Walk on this road.
26	1.61	38,51,59N	107,0,17W	9,401'	Leave old 4x4 road. Continue on subdivision road.
27	2.04	38,51,42N	107,0,21W	9,565'	Leave subdivision road. Start on trail again.
28	4.2	38,50,40N	107,1,49W	10,598'	Green Lake.

View of Crested Butte

Gothic Valley

The Gothic Valley is Crested Butte's wildflower showcase. The combination of fertile soil, rain, and sun produce an astounding variety of species and color. Though the other valleys also have wildflowers in abundance, they don't have such a variety in such density. If you want wildflowers, go to the Gothic Valley hikes.

The 2-wheel drive dirt road (CR 317) is a favorite for local mountain bikers and provides access for outdoor enthusiasts to numerous free camping sites and to twenty-one of the hiking

trails included in this book. The valley road climbs gently past the 1880's mining town of Gothic (home to The Rocky Mountain Biological Laboratory that studies high altitude plants), past Emerald Lake to Schofield Pass. Dropping down the other side into Schofield Park (the extinct 1879 town site for silver miners), the road follows the original 1880 toll road through the infamous Devil's Punchbowl (4x4) through Crystal Canyon, and finally settles in Marble.

View of Gothic Valley from Hike 16

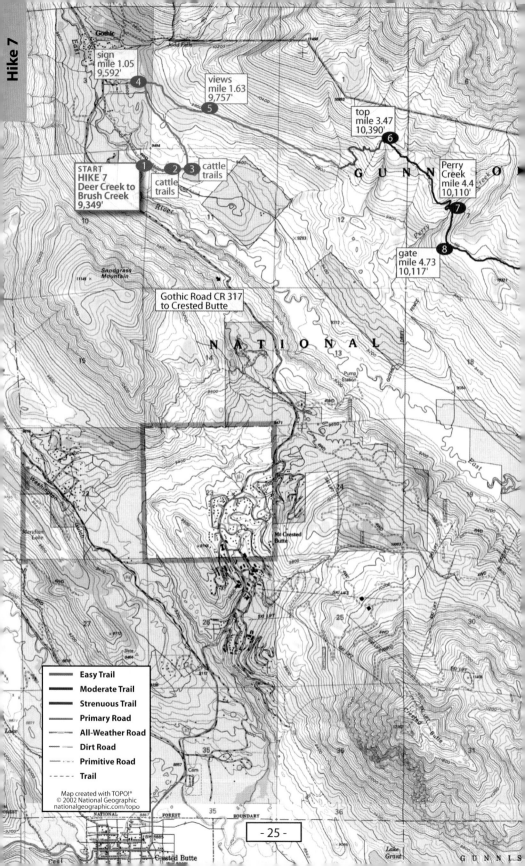

sign
mile 1.05
9,592'

4

views
mile 1.63
9,757'

5

top
mile 3.47
10,390'

6

Perry
Creek
mile 4.4
10,110'

7

1 **2** **3** cattle
trails

cattle
trails

START
HIKE 7
Deer Creek to
Brush Creek
9,349'

gate
mile 4.73
10,117'

8

G U N N

River

Gothic Road CR 317
to Crested Butte

N A T I O N A L

Mt Crested
Butte

	Easy Trail
	Moderate Trail
	Strenuous Trail
	Primary Road
	All-Weather Road
	Dirt Road
	Primitive Road
	Trail

G U N N I S

FOLLOW THE GPS POINTS

Hike 7 - Deer Creek to Brush Creek, 1-5, **6-11, SHUTTLE**

gate/enter forest
mile 6.7 10,462'

10

to Teocali Ridge

11 END
HIKE 7
mile 8.23
9,698'

to Deer Creek TH

few turnouts
one lane road
to West Brush Creek

to Pearl Pass

to Crested Butte
via CR 738 & 135

MILES

0   0.5   1

Deer Creek to
7 Brush Creek

Distance	8.23 from start to shuttle point.
Difficulty Rating	Moderate with two short steep sections.
Surface	Mostly easy packed dirt.
Gradient	Easy first 2.8 miles. Steep for 0.67 miles. Moderate for 4.64 miles.
Average Time	5 hours.
Elevations	TH: 9,349; Highest: 10,462; Gain: +1,902
Maps	Latitude 40 Crested Butte, Taylor Park; Trails Illustrated #131. Trail 568
Star Rating	☆☆☆☆

Approximate route of trail

Highlights

Reach out and touch White Rock Mountain as the trail passes along the base, Wide open meadows with views of Gothic Mountain, and the Crested Butte Ski Area. Wonderful seasonal wildflowers and fall aspen color. Not heavily traveled. Go out & back as far as you wish.

Directions To Trailhead: From CBVC, drive 7.5 miles north on Gothic Road CR 317. Just after the East River Bridge, there is a signed dirt road to the right (SE). Drive SUV 0.75 miles up this narrow public road to the trailhead sign. Pass through two gates. There is parking just before the trailhead sign.

Shuttle: From CBVC, drive 2.07 miles south on CO 135 to Brush Creek Road. Turn left (NE) and drive 5.61 miles on paved then gravel road to marked junction. Follow West Brush Creek Road. From this point, the road is only one vehicle wide. Follow signs to Deer Creek Trailhead another 2.14 miles.

Trail Description

The trail starts out easy, passing through a pasture area with cattle trails. Do not take the first cattle trail left. The real trail is the second left ❸. After this turn north, there are several intersecting cattle trails beyond, but always follow the larger trail. Enter aspen forest in a little less than a mile until mile 1.63 ❺, where the landscape opens up to expansive views. At the top of the climb ❻, you feel close enough to reach out and touch White Rock Mountain as it rises dramatically from the surrounding meadows.

The best views are in the first half of the hike. A good turnaround point is before dropping into Perry Creek, at about mile 4.0 ❼. After mile 6.7 ❿, the views diminish dramatically as the trail enters a forested drainage. If you prefer not to make the long shuttle, you might consider turning around and hiking back to the starting point, instead.

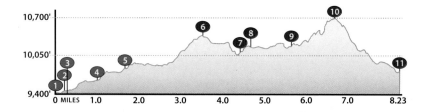

Gothic Mountain

Crested Butte Mountain

GPS	Mile	Latitude	Longitude	Elevation	Comment
1	0.0	38,56,45N	106,58,53W	9,349'	Start Deer Creek to Brush Creek.
2	0.2	38,56,44N	106,58,39W	9,425'	Cattle trail crosses. Go straight ahead.
3	0.3	38,56,44N	106,58,34W	9,423'	Cattle trail. Hikers go left (N).
4	1.05	38,57,18N	106,58,56W	9,592'	Deer Creek Trail sign.
5	1.63	38,57,7N	106,58,24W	9,757'	Leave aspen forest. Views.
6	3.47	38,56,55N	106,56,49W	10,390'	Top of hill.
7	4.40	38,56,29N	106,56,14W	10,110'	Perry Creek.
8	4.73	38,56,13N	106,56,14W	10,117'	Fence with gate.
9	5.65	38,56,6N	106,55,19W	10,151'	Creek.
10	6.70	38,55,38N	106,54,32W	10,462'	Gate. Soon enter spruce.
11	8.23	38,55,5N	106,53,36W	9,698'	Finish Deer Creek Trail.

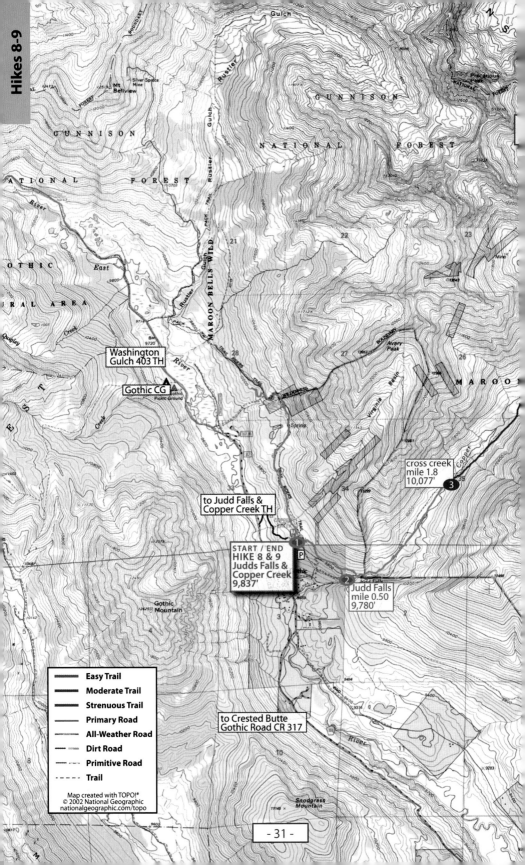

Washington
Gulch 403 TH

Gothic CG

to Judd Falls &
Copper Creek TH

cross creek
mile 1.8
10,077'
3

START / END
HIKE 8 & 9
Judds Falls &
Copper Creek
9,837'
1

2 Judd Falls
mile 0.50
9,780'

to Crested Butte
Gothic Road CR 317

Easy Trail
Moderate Trail
Strenuous Trail
Primary Road
All-Weather Road
Dirt Road
Primitive Road
Trail

Map created with TOPO!®
© 2002 National Geographic
nationalgeographic.com/topo

FOLLOW THE GPS POINTS

Hike 8 - Judd Falls, 1,2, RETURN

Hike 9 - Copper Creek, 1-8, RETURN

junction
mile 4.6
11,418'

ss creek: shoes
e 3.5   10,561'

creek: shoes
.3   10,531'

MILES

0   0.5   1

Judd Falls

Judd Falls

Distance	1.0 mile out & back.
Difficulty Rating	Easy.
Surface	Very rocky.
Gradient	Easy.
Average Time	45 minutes.
Elevations	TH: 9,837; Highest: 9,904; Gain: +67
Maps	Latitude 40 Crested Butte, Taylor Park. Trail 983

Star Rating

Highlights

This is an easy trail with views of Gothic Mountain and Judd Falls.

Directions To Trailhead: From CBVC, drive 8.45 miles north on Gothic Road CR 317 to the signed Copper Creek parking area. Drive SUV 0.5 miles further to an upper parking area. If you cannot drive this road, add 1.0 mile out & back to the hike.

Trail Description

This is a popular trail close to town. It is a very short, rocky trail that passes through aspen forest to a waterfall. There are some good views of Gothic Mountain.

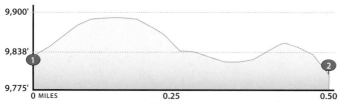

Rocky route

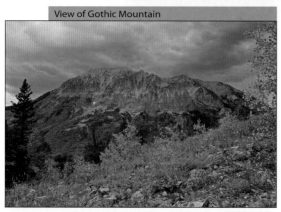

View of Gothic Mountain

GPS	Mile	Latitude	Longitude	Elevation	Comment
1	0.0	38,57,50N	106,59,17W	9,837'	Start Judd Falls from upper parking area.
2	0.50	38,57,35N	106,58,53W	9,780'	Judd Falls.

Copper Creek

Distance	10.4 miles out & back.
	(River crossing shoes recommended.)
Difficulty Rating	Moderate.
Surface	Very rocky most of the way.
Gradient	Easy to mile 3.5. Moderate from 3.5 to the lake .
Average Time	7 hours.
Elevations	TH: 9,837; Highest: 11,893; Gain: +2,163
Maps	Latitude 40 Crested Butte, Taylor Park. Trail 983
Star Rating	

Copper Lake viewed from pass

Highlights

From Copper Lake to East Maroon Pass, the views are spectacular. Towering granite peaks form a cirque around the very picturesque lake. In season, wildflowers near the pass are thick and colorful.

Directions To Trailhead: From CBVC, drive 8.45 miles north on Gothic Road CR 317 to the signed Copper Creek parking area. Drive SUV 0.5 miles further to an upper parking area. If you cannot drive this road, add 1.0 mile out & back to the hike.

Trail Description

Copper Creek is one of the most popular hikes in the Crested Butte area, as it is close to town and has a classic cirque mountain lake as the destination. Overnight campers make an additional loop around Conundrum and East Maroon Pass.

The trail meanders over, through, and around rocky mounds all the way to Judd Falls. After the falls, the trail follows an old four wheel drive road to the lake. The road is easy packed dirt and ascends gradually from Judd Falls to the first stream crossing at mile 1.8 **3**. This crossing, as well as two more **4 & 5**, require changing to wet shoes. In springtime, these crossings can be dangerous because of the depth and force of the water.

After crossing the stream for the first time, the old road enters very dense spruce forest, and the surface changes from packed dirt to loose rock. It gets steeper, with more broken rock clogging the road all the way to the lake. About the only views along the entire route come when you cross the streams and can see up valley. There are also occasional views of Gothic Mountain on the return trip.

Copper Lake is very picturesque **7**. The most scenic part of the entire hike is the trail that goes from Copper Lake to East Maroon Pass **7 to 8**. The ascending trail looks down on the classic cirque lake. From the vantage point of the high pass, you are face to face with the massive granite walls of White Rock Mountain, which have been at your side all day long but hidden from view by the dense forest.

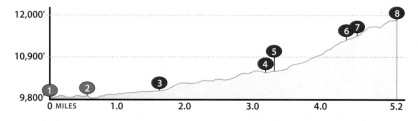

White Rock Mountain from Pass

Wildflowers at Pass

GPS	Mile	Latitude	Longitude	Elevation	Comment
1	0.0	38,57,50N	106,59,17W	9,837'	Start Copper Creek at upper parking area.
2	0.50	38,57,35N	106,58,53W	9,780'	Judd Falls.
3	1.8	38,58,14N	106.57.56W	10,077'	Cross Copper Creek. Wet shoes.
4	3.3	38,59,10N	106,56,54W	10,531'	Cross Copper Creek. Wet shoes.
5	3.5	38,59,17N	106,56,47W	10,561'	Cross Copper Creek. Wet shoes.
6	4.4	39,0,0N	106,56,30W	11,319'	Junction: Triangle Pass Trail.
7	4.6	39,0,12N	106,56,24W	11,481'	Copper Lake. Junction: to East Maroon Pass.
8	5.2	39,0,40N	106,56,29W	11,893'	East Maroon Pass.

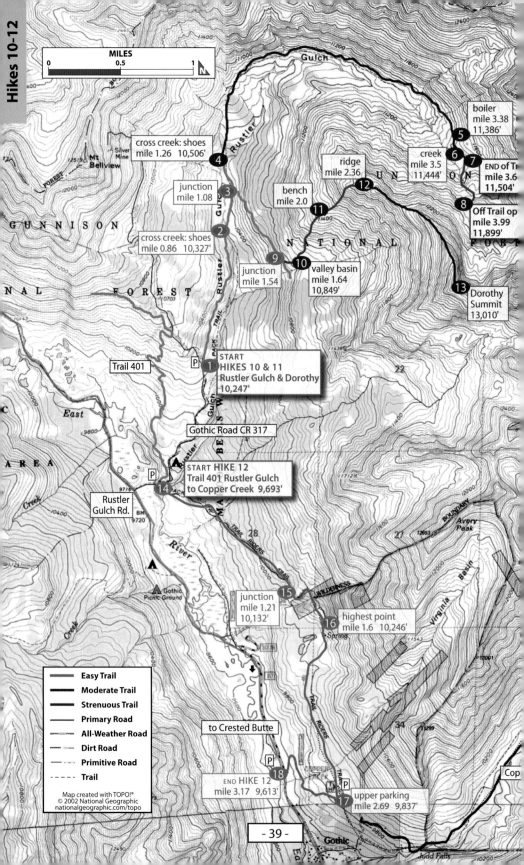

MILES

0   0.5   1

cross creek: shoes
mile 1.26 10,506'

4

Silver
Mine

Mt
Bellview

junction
mile 1.08

3

ridge
mile 2.36

creek
mile 3.5
11,444'

boiler
mile 3.38
11,386'

5

6

7

END of Tr
mile 3.6
11,504'

bench
mile 2.0

12

8

Off Trail op
mile 3.99
11,899'

G U N N I S O N

11

cross creek: shoes
mile 0.86 10,327'

2

F O R E S T

N A T I O N A L

9

10

valley basin
mile 1.64
10,849'

junction
mile 1.54

13

Dorothy
Summit
13,010'

N
A
L

F O R E S T

Trail 401

P

1

START
HIKES 10 & 11
Rustler Gulch & Dorothy
10,247'

East

Gothic Road CR 317

P

START HIKE 12
Trail 401 Rustler Gulch
to Copper Creek 9,693'

14

Rustler
Gulch Rd.

BM
9720

9716

River

BOUNDARY

Avery
Peak

Gothic
Picnic Ground

junction
mile 1.21
10,132'

15

WILDERNESS

16

highest point
mile 1.6 10,246'

Virginia
Basin

Spring

to Crested Butte

P

18

END HIKE 12
mile 3.17 9,613'

Cop

17

upper parking
mile 2.69 9,837'

Gothic

Judd Falls

- 39 -

Easy Trail

Moderate Trail

Strenuous Trail

Primary Road

All-Weather Road

Dirt Road

Primitive Road

Trail

Map created with TOPO!®
© 2002 National Geographic
nationalgeographic.com/topo

FOLLOW THE GPS POINTS

Hike 10 - Rustler Gulch,1-8, RETURN

Hike 11 - Dorothy Peak ,1-3, 9-13, RETURN

Hike 12 - Trail 401: Rustler Gulch to Copper Creek TH. ,14-18, SHUTTLE

Rustler Gulch

Distance	7.0 (or 7.98) miles out & back.
	(River crossing shoes recommended.)
Difficulty Rating	Moderate. (Beyond is difficult.)
Surface	Alternating easy packed dirt with rocky terrain. (Beyond is meadows.)
Gradient	Easy to moderate. (Beyond is very steep.)
Average Time	4 hours, 30 minutes. (Beyond is 6 hours, 30 minutes.)
Elevations	TH: 10,247; Highest: 11,444 (or 11,899); Gain: +1,302 (or +1,757)
Maps	Latitude 40 Crested Butte, Taylor Park;
	Trails Illustrated #128 & #133. Trail 599
Star Rating	

View from high point of extended hike

Highlights

Rustler Gulch is a showcase for the astonishing variety of seasonal wildflowers that prosper in the Gothic Valley. Rustler Creek tumbles through the midst of these flowered meadows. Waterfalls plummet straight down from the massive rock cliffs. Precarious Peak, at the end of the wide valley, creates a semi-circle barrier of sharp, jagged grey granite. Outstanding views of Gothic Mountain, Mount Bellview, and Avery Peak.

Directions To Trailhead: From CBVC, drive 10.41 miles north on Gothic Road CR 317. Turn right (NE) at the signed Rustler Gulch Road. Cars can drive the 0.2-mile rocky road to the East River. Cross the river (check depth) and park on the east side, or continue driving (SUV) up the very steep, narrow road 1 mile to the trailhead sign. There is parking for about five vehicles. If you do not drive up to the trailhead sign, you must add 2 miles out and back to the length of the hike and 566 feet of elevation gain.

Trail Description

You are already surrounded by flower meadows with views of Gothic Mountain and Avery Peak when you start this hike. A very brief saunter through spruce forest quickly returns to meadows. The first creek crossing requiring wet shoes is at mile 0.86 **2** . The second is at mile 1.26 **4** . After the second creek, the hardest part of the trail, very rocky and a little steeper, leads up close to the jagged red rocks that have been your view. You are starting on the long gradual curve of the trail that shows prominently on the map. As you progress, views of Precarious Peak and the whole valley spread out in front like a colorful painting. We recommend going up as far as mile 3.5, where you cross Rustler Creek at a series of small, photogenic waterfalls **6** .

The trail continues beyond the creek for just a bit before disappearing **7** . If you wish to hike on, make your own switchbacks up the wide grassy slope on the west side of the red rock moraine to the first bench. To go higher, climb up the very steep grassy slope close to the red moraine. If you make this extra effort, the views down valley are superior **8** .

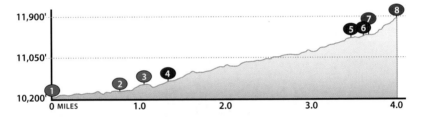

Start of hike with Gothic Mountain

View up valley near corner

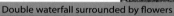
View down valley from corner

Double waterfall surrounded by flowers

Recommended turnaround at waterfall

GPS	Mile	Latitude	Longitude	Elevation	Comment
1	0.0	38,59,58N	107,0,11W	10,247'	Start Rustler Gulch.
2	0.86	39,0,38N	107,0,2W	10,327'	Rustler Creek. Wet shoes.
3	1.08	39,0,49N	107,0,0W	10,476'	Junction: to Dorothy Peak.
4	1.26	39,0,58N	107,0,4W	10,506'	Rustler Creek. Wet shoes.
5	3.38	39,1,6N	106,58,29W	11,386'	Old mining boiler.
6	3.50	39,1,1N	106,58,27W	11,444'	Rustler Creek waterfalls. Turnaround.
7	3.66	39,0,58N	106,58,24W	11,504'	Trail ends suddenly.
8	3.99	39,0,46N	106,58,23W	11,899'	End optional extension of hike.

Dorothy Peak

Distance	6.48 miles out & back.
	(River crossing shoes recommended.)
Difficulty Rating	Difficult.
Surface	Difficult cross country through thick vegetation to get to the ridge.
Gradient	Very steep to get to the ridge.
Average Time	7 hours.
Elevations	TH: 10,247; Highest: 13,010; Gain: +2,624
Maps	Latitude 40 Crested Butte, Taylor Park. Trail 599 & off trail.
Star Rating	

Summit

Highlights

This is a long, moderate ridgeline once you get to it. There are stupendous views of rugged Precarious Peak, all of Rustler Gulch, Mount Bellview, Gothic Mountain, Mount Baldy, and the list goes on. This is an adventure, not a hike.

Directions To Trailhead: From CBVC, drive 10.41 miles north on Gothic Road CR 317. Turn right (NE) at the signed Rustler Gulch Road. Cars can drive the 0.2-mile rocky road to the East River. Cross the river (check depth) and park on the east side, or continue driving (SUV) up the very steep, narrow road 1 mile to the trailhead sign. There is parking for about five vehicles. If you do not drive up to the trailhead sign, you must add 2 miles out and back to the length of the hike and 566 feet of elevation gain.

Trail Description

This is actually a climb to an unnamed peak affectionately referred to as Dorothy by the locals. There is no easy route to Dorothy's ridge. You have to scramble up the thickly vegetated and very steep hillside to get there.

From the Rustler Gulch Trailhead, hike 0.86 miles on the easy trail to Rustler Creek **2** . You may need crossing shoes through the end of August. If you scout downstream a hundred yards, there is a big tree across the stream. Savvy hikers have made a trail to it. After crossing the stream, continue following Rustler Gulch Trail another 0.22 miles to an unmarked junction **3** . Take the lesser trail up to the right (SE).

Along this trail, keep your eyes open for another left hand spur at mile 1.54 **9** . Take this smaller trail left (E) uphill. In less than 0.1 miles, it will lead you to the valley basin **10** . If you miss this spur, the main trail will head into the thickets and get lost in a muddy creek very soon. Just turn back about 50 feet and scramble up the short grassy slope to the basin.

Once in the basin, you can see the formidable task in front of you—climbing to the northern ridgeline **11** . The wildflowers are tall and thick and smother the very steep slopes. Head a little bit left (NW) towards the trees, then hike up parallel to them. When you finally reach the rocky ridge **12** , it is a moderate trek to the summit **13** , which is the second highest in the Crested Butte area (Treasury Mountain is the tallest). The summit is a tiny, rocky bump with views to kill for. What an accomplishment!

It is possible to walk down (or up) the south ridgeline. It is steeper than the route we describe, and there is a lot of loose rock according to locals. We did not hike this route, so we cannot describe it accurately.

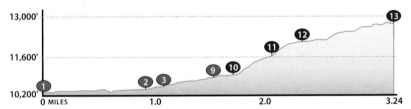

View behind

Route from basin to ridge

P E A K

Hiking up the ridgeline

GPS	Mile	Latitude	Longitude	Elevation	Comment
1	0.0	38,59,58N	107,0,11W	10,247'	Start Dorothy Peak.
2	0.86	39,0,38N	107,0,2W	10,327'	Cross Rustler Creek. Wet shoes.
3	1.08	39,0,49N	107,0,0W	10,476'	Unmarked junction: turn right (SE).
9	1.54	39,0,30N	106,59,40W	10,788'	Take left fork uphill (east).
10	1.64	39,0,29N	106,59,34W	10,849'	Bottom of valley basin.
11	2.0	39,0,43N	106,59,22W	11,474'	First bench along ridge.
12	2.36	39,0,51N	106,59,6W	12,099'	Ridge.
13	3.24	39,0,22N	106,58,28W	13,010'	Summit Dorothy Peak.

Trail 401: Rustler Gulch to Copper Creek TH.

Distance	3.17 miles from start to shuttle point.
Difficulty Rating	Easy.
Surface	Easy packed dirt.
Gradient	Easy.
Average Time	2 hours.
Elevations	TH: 9,693; Highest: 10,246; Gain: +566; Loss: -676
Maps	Latitude 40 Crested Butte, Taylor Park. Trail 401 (Trailriders)
Star Rating	

Avery Peak

Highlights

An easy trail ascending and descending a wide, sunny valley surrounded by dramatic peaks. Wildflowers in season. Beaver ponds.

Directions To Trailhead: From CBVC, drive north 10.41 miles on Gothic Road CR 317 to signed Rustler Gulch Road. Cars can drive 0.2 miles down this rocky road. Drive across stream (check depth) and park on the east side. There is a trailhead sign.

Shuttle: From CBVC, drive north 8.45 miles on Gothic Road CR 317 to signed trailhead for Judd Falls and Copper Lake. Park at lower lot.

Trail Description

This is not a heavily traveled trail. It passes through a mix of open meadows and heavily forested areas of aspen and spruce. There are very picturesque beaver ponds and views of Gothic Mountain. Avery Peak also comes into view at several locations.

An old 4x4 road from Avery Picnic Area intersects the trail at mile 1.21 **15**, and 401 follows this route for a distance. The last section follows a 4x4 road from the Judd Falls trailhead to Gothic Road. Overall, this is a very pleasant short hike. The gradient is gentle, and the surface is mostly smooth.

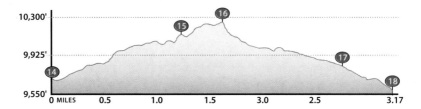

GPS	Mile	Latitude	Longitude	Elevation	Comment
14	0.0	38,59,23N	107,0,29W	9,693'	Start Trail 401 Rustler Gulch to Copper Creek.
15	1.21	38,58,51N	106,59,35W	10,132'	Road to Avery Picnic Area.
16	1.60	38,58,42N	106,59,22W	10,246'	Highest elevation point.
17	2.69	38,57,50N	106,59,17W	9,837'	Junction: Judd Falls TH.
18	3.17	38,57,58N	106,59,38W	9,613'	Finish hike on Gothic Road.

Views across valley

Beaver ponds

Views of Crested Butte Mountain

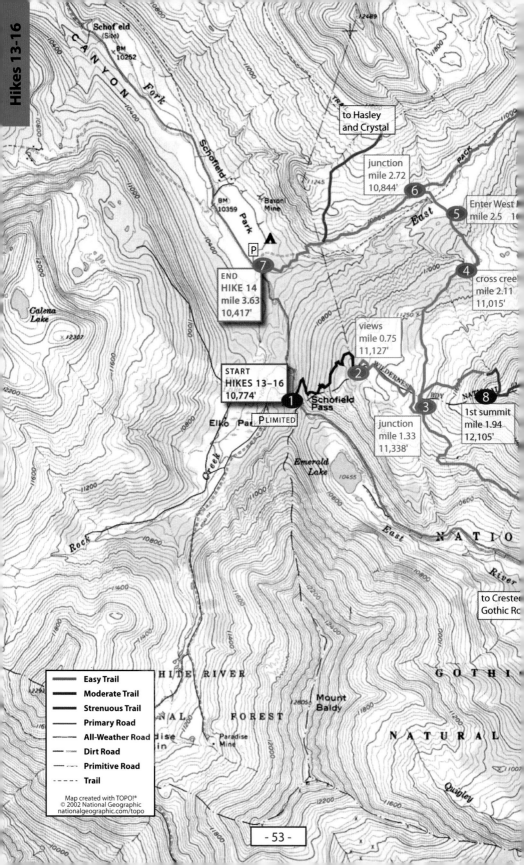

to Hasley
and Crystal

junction
mile 2.72
10,844' **6**

5 Enter West N
mile 2.5   10

4 cross creek
mile 2.11
11,015'

7

END
HIKE 14
mile 3.63
10,417'

views
mile 0.75
11,127'

2

START
HIKES 13–16
10,774'

1 Schofield
Pass

junction
mile 1.33
11,338'

3

8

1st summit
mile 1.94
12,105'

Emerald
Lake

to Crested
Gothic Ro

Mount
Baldy

Easy Trail
Moderate Trail
Strenuous Trail
Primary Road
All-Weather Road
Dirt Road
Primitive Road
Trail

Map created with TOPO!®
© 2002 National Geographic
nationalgeographic.com/topo

FOLLOW THE GPS POINTS

Hike 13 - Trail 401: Schofield Pass to Viewpoint, 1-3, RETURN

Hike 14 - Trail 401: Schofield Pass to West Maroon, 1-7, SHUTTLE

Hike 15 - Trail 401: Schofield Pass to Mount Bellview, 1-3, 8-10 RETURN

Hike 16 - Trail 401: Schofield Pass to Rustler Gulch. , 1-3, 11-12, SHUTTLE

10 Mt Bellview
mile 2.72
12,519'

Rustler Gulch Trail

11 Users sign
mile 3.4
10,627'

12 END
HIKE 16
mile 5.17 9,706'

Rustler Gulch Road

MILES
0   0.5   1

Trail 401

Trail 401: Schofield Pass to Viewpoint

Hikers approach viewpoint

Distance	2.66 miles out & back.
Difficulty Rating	Easy to Moderate.
Surface	Easy packed dirt all the way.
Gradient	Sustained difficult first 0.75 miles. Easy to turnaround point.
Average Time	2 hours, 15 minutes.
Elevations	TH: 10,774; Highest: 11,338; Gain: +660
Maps	Latitude 40 Crested Butte, Taylor Park; Trails Illustrated #128. Trail 401

Star Rating ☆☆☆☆☆

GPS	Mile	Latitude	Longitude	Elevation	Comment
1	0.0	39,0,55N	107,2,49W	10,774′	Trail 401: Schofield Pass to Viewpoint.
2	0.75	39,1,3N	107,2,29W	11,127′	Exit spruce. Spectacular vistas.
3	1.33	39,0,53N	107,2,9W	11,338′	Summit Trail 401. Turnaround.

Highlights

Walk through healthy spruce forest with thick wildflower under-story. Arrive quickly at high elevation vistas. See the Maroon Bells, the Ragged Range, Frigid Air Pass, Hasley Pass, Mount Bellview, and Mount Baldy. You are completely surrounded by peaks. Seasonal, summer wildflowers explode across the vast hillsides. For a short hike with easy access, this is spectacular.

Spruce and wildflowers

Directions To Trailhead: From CBVC, drive north 13.37 miles on Gothic Road CR 317. SUVs are recommended beyond mile 12. The road gets very narrow with high cliffs. The trailhead sign is at the summit of Schofield Pass. Parking is limited.

Mount Bellview and wildflowers

Trail Description

Trail 401 is extremely popular with mountain bikers. You will certainly meet them along the route. The trail begins with an upward thrust that twists through healthy spruce forest blessed with a colorful seasonal under-story of wildflowers. True to Gothic Valley fame, they grow waist high, in the forest as well as across the sunny meadows.

By mile 0.75 **2**, this peaceful, colorful forest has given way to explosive vistas of mountain ranges all the way to the summit, where there is a trail junction **3**. This is your turnaround point. The trail leading northwest connects with the West Maroon Trail 1970 (hike 14). The trail to the right (SE) goes down Gothic Valley to Rustler Gulch Trailhead (hike 16).

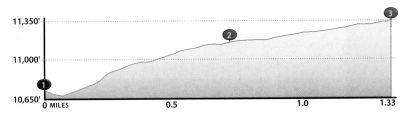

Trail 401: Schofield Pass to West Maroon

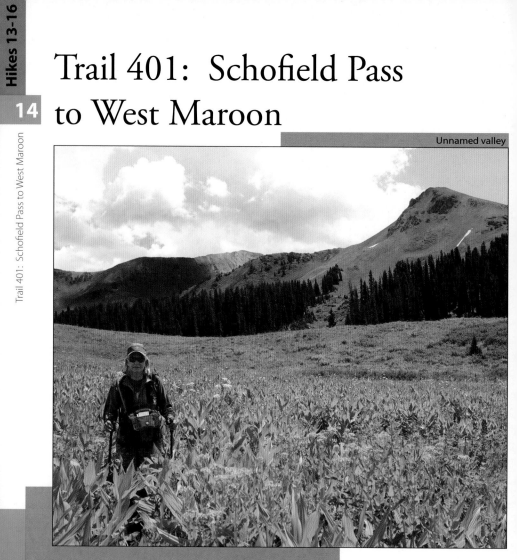

Unnamed valley

Distance	3.64 miles with shuttle.
	4.25 miles if walking entire loop.
Difficulty Rating	Easy to Moderate.
Surface	Mostly easy packed dirt.
Gradient	Easy except for first 0.75 miles, which is difficult.
Average Time	2 hours, 30 minutes with shuttle; 3 hours walking entire loop.
Elevations	TH: 10,774; Highest: 11,338; Gain: +741; Loss: - 1,036
Maps	Latitude 40 Crested Butte, Taylor Park; Trails Illustrated 128.
	Trail 401 to 1970
Star Rating	

Highlights

Walk through healthy spruce forest with wondrous displays of wildflowers growing waist high beneath the canopy. Vistas of the Ruby Range and the Maroon Bells explode across the horizon. Meadows smothered in seasonal wildflowers frame the view. Mount Bellview looms above. Enter an unnamed valley thick with wildflowers.

> **Directions To Trailhead:** From CBVC, drive north 13.37 miles on Gothic Road CR 317. SUVs are recommended beyond mile 12. The road gets very narrow with high cliffs. The trailhead sign is at the summit of Schofield Pass. Parking is limited.

Views midway along trail

Trail Description

Read the description for hike 13 to ③ . Then follow below.

From the summit, take the trail leading northwest. Soon, you will see the registration box for the Wilderness area. Bikes are not permitted beyond this sign. The trail contours around the flower-covered slopes of Mount Bellview, opening various vistas of the Ruby Range. The expansiveness is overwhelming. Cross a small gully cutting through the bench land. Soon after, the trail descends into a small valley. Compared to the expansive views, it is intimate. Drop steeply into a stream ④ . Once you climb out, you enter a completely new valley. The trail nearly gets lost in the waist high seasonal flowers. It seems nobody has ever been here before. Then the trail enters spruce forest for a short, moderate trek downhill. When you emerge, you enter the West Maroon Valley ⑤ .

You may not see the West Maroon Trail hidden in the flowered hillside across the way, but you may see hikers' heads bobbing along. You want to intersect that trail. Meanwhile, your trail has mostly disappeared, and Crystal Creek separates you from your goal. Look up valley a few hundred feet, and you will spot a flat approach to the creek and a shallower place to cross (You may need wet shoes). Work your

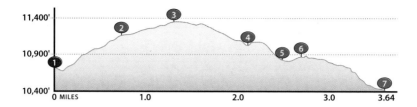

Ascending to first open meadow

way through the vegetation and intersect the trail ⑥ . From there, it is 1 mile to the finish. If you do not have a shuttle vehicle, there are many friendly hikers driving their cars back to town. It may be possible to get a ride. Otherwise, it is about 0.61 miles uphill on the road to meet your car at Schofield Pass.

Descending towards smaller valley

GPS	Mile	Latitude	Longitude	Elevation	Comment
1	0.0	39,0,55N	107,2,49W	10,774'	Start Trail 401 Schofield Pass to West Maroon Trail.
2	0.75	39,1,3N	107,2,29W	11,127'	Exit spruce. Spectacular mountain vistas.
3	1.33	39,0,53N	107,2,9W	11,338'	Summit Trail 401. Junction. Go left (N).
4	2.11	39,1,29N	107,1,53W	11,015'	Deep gully. Cross stream.
5	2.50	39,1,43N	107,1,58W	10,840'	Enter West Maroon Valley.
6	2.72	39,1,48N	107,2,10W	10,844'	Junction with West Maroon Trail. No sign.
7	3.63	39,1,29N	107,3,0W	10,417'	End hike at West Maroon TH.

Trail 401: Schofield Pass to Mount Bellview

Route from wilderness sign to Mount Bellview

Distance	5.56 miles out & back.
Difficulty Rating	Difficult from summit of Trail 401.
Surface	Easy packed dirt to 401 summit. No trail beyond.
Gradient	Moderate to 401 summit. Very steep beyond.
Average Time	6 hours.
Elevations	TH: 10,774; Highest: 12,519; Gain: + 2,023
Maps	Latitude 40 Crested Butte, Taylor Park; Trails Illustrated #128. Trail 401
Star Rating	

Highlights

This is an off-trail climb to a peak with multiple, varied, and classic Colorado high elevation vistas. Hiking the narrow ridge out to Mount Bellview is an adventure.

Directions To Trailhead: From CBVC, drive north 13.37 miles on Gothic Road CR 317. SUVs are recommended beyond mile 12. The road gets very narrow with high cliffs. The trailhead sign is at the summit of Schofield Pass. Parking is limited.

Trail Description

Read the description for hike 13 to ③ , then follow below.

From the summit of Trail 401, take the trail leading northwest. When you get to the registration box for the Wilderness area, stand facing it and look north to the two rounded peaks. Your first goal is reach the saddle between those peaks.

From the box, walk up slope directly towards the first peak. There are three gullies to your left. You want to get above them. Once above the gullies, you can see the saddle clearly. Contour around the north side of the peaks. Look for a large rock outcropping about halfway up. A long, deep gully extends directly below these rocks. Cross between the high point of the gully and those rocks. Once past the rocks, it is a steep uphill climb straight towards the saddle ⑧ . Views of the surrounding ranges are spectacular. For some hikers, this is a great place to turn around.

For those continuing, the trek up the very steep, rocky slope to the second summit ⑨ takes about 30 minutes. The rock is soft enough for good footing. There is even a faint trail carved by other hikers. The top is about 30 feet wide. Due east is Mt. Bellview summit ⑩. It is at the end of a steep ridgeline that is only 18 inches wide in places. The trail leading out on this 0.58-mile route is evidence of use by hikers. Be aware of the weather before making a decision. You are exposed to strong winds and lightning. Once on this ridge, there is no place safe to hide. Leave time to descend.

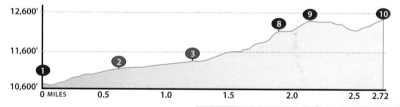

View from first summit

GPS	Mile	Latitude	Longitude	Elevation	Comment
1	0.0	39,0,55N	107,2,49W	10,774'	Start Trail 401 Schofield Pass to Mt. Bellview.
2	0.75	39,1,3N	107,2,29W	11,127'	Exit spruce. Spectacular mountain vistas.
3	1.33	39,0,53N	107,2,9W	11,338'	Summit Trail 401. Junction. Go left (N).
8	1.94	39,0,56N	107,1,43W	12,105'	First summit.
9	2.14	39,0,59N	107,1,31W	12,369'	Second summit.
10	2.72	39,0,58N	107,1,0W	12,519	Mt. Bellview summit.

Views while climbing towards the saddle

Ascending to second summit

View from second summit

Trail 401: Schofield Pass to Rustler Gulch

Distance	5.17 miles from start to shuttle point.
Difficulty Rating	Easy. (0.75 miles of difficult at start)
Surface	Mostly easy packed dirt.
Gradient	All easy downhill except for first 1.33 miles.
Average Time	3 hours, 30 minutes.
Elevations	TH: 10,774; Highest: 11,338; Gain: +658; Loss: -1,676
Maps	Latitude 40 Crested Butte, Taylor Park;
	Trails Illustrated 128 &131. Trail 401
Star Rating	

Views up valley

Highlights

An easy trail ascending and descending This is the best of both worlds. High elevation views with a downhill walk most of the way. See the Maroon Bells, the Ragged Range, Frigid Air Pass, Hasley Pass, Mount Bellview, Mount Baldy, Gothic Mountain, Avery Peak, and down the Gothic Valley to Crested Butte. Summer wildflowers explode across the vast hillsides.

Directions To Trailhead: From CBVC, drive north 13.37 miles on Gothic Road CR 317. SUVs are recommended beyond mile 12. The road gets very narrow with high cliffs. The trailhead sign is at the summit of Schofield Pass. Parking is limited.

Shuttle: From CBVC, drive north 10.41 miles on Gothic Road CR 317 to signed Rustler Gulch Road. Cars can drive 0.2 miles down this rocky road. Drive across the stream and park there. If you cannot drive across, bring wet shoes for wading it.

Trail Description

Read the description for hike 13 to ③ , then continue below.

At the summit of 401, turn right (SE) and begin the easy descent all the way to Rustler's Gulch. The trail hangs high on the flank of Mount Bellview. The views down Gothic Valley and up the valley to Schofield Pass persist across endless hillsides smothered in seasonal wildflowers.

Just after mile 3.4 ⑪ , a tiny Forest Service sign designates who can legally use this trail A little further on, you might see a road above and to your left. That is the Bellview Mine Road that eventually intersects with Rustler Gulch Road. There are no signs. Nobody goes that way anymore since a new trail heads downhill into a beautiful grove of aspens and flowers. Follow this route downhill. In less than 2 miles, you will meet Rustler Gulch Road. Go down this steep road for just 0.13 miles to your car.

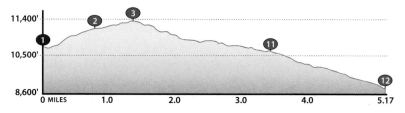

GPS	Mile	Latitude	Longitude	Elevation	Comment
1	0.0	39,0,55N	107,2,49W	10,774'	Start Trail 401 Schofield Pass to Rustler Gulch.
2	0.75	39,1,3N	107,2,29W	11,127'	Exit spruce. Spectacular mountain vistas.
3	1.33	39,0,53N	107,2,9W	11,338'	Summit Trail 401. Junction. Go right (SE).
11	3.40	39,0,12N	107,0,29W	10,627'	Trail 401 sign designating legal users.
12	5.17	38,59,23N	107,0,29W	9,706'	End Trail 401 to Rustler Gulch.

Looking down Gothic Valley

Ascending to first meadow

View from summit of Trail 401

Technical section for bike

to Crystal

junction
mile 5.84
10,455' **13**

14 ponds
mile 6.46
10,487'

junction
mile 5.68
9,556' **6**

cross creek
mile 4.36
11,191' **5**

7 END
HIKE 18
mile 6.7
9,167'

junction
12,040'

junction
mile 2.35
11,521' **4**

junction
11,985' **12**

16

4 mile suttle
Jeep or ATV

Hasley Pass
mile 3.15
12,121' **11**

junction **10**

9

junction
mile 1.37
11,511' **3**

junction
mile 1.31
10,908' **8**

START
HIKES 17–23
West Maroon
Trail System
10,417' **1**

2 junction
mile 0.53
10,690'

	Easy Trail
	Moderate Trail
	Strenuous Trail
	Primary Road
	All-Weather Road
	Dirt Road
	Primitive Road
	Trail

Map created with TOPO!®
© 2002 National Geographic
nationalgeographic.com/topo

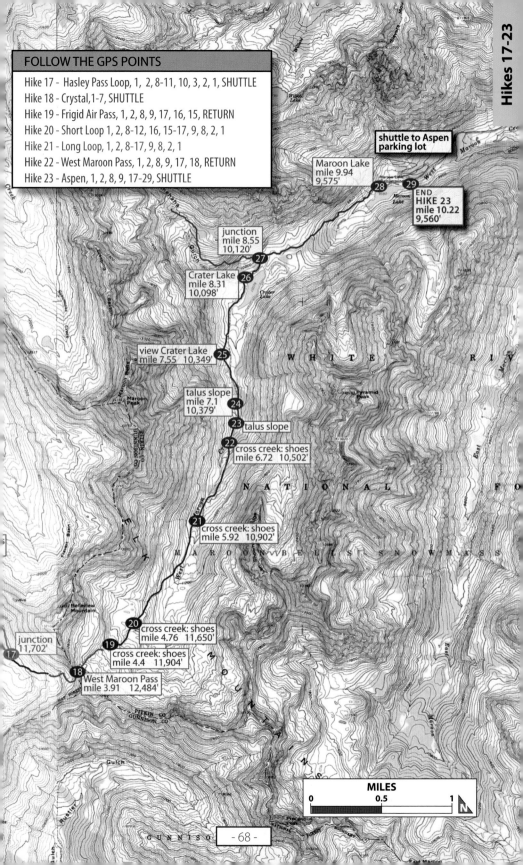

FOLLOW THE GPS POINTS

Hike 17 - Hasley Pass Loop, 1, 2, 8-11, 10, 3, 2, 1, SHUTTLE
Hike 18 - Crystal, 1-7, SHUTTLE
Hike 19 - Frigid Air Pass, 1, 2, 8, 9, 17, 16, 15, RETURN
Hike 20 - Short Loop 1, 2, 8-12, 16, 15-17, 9, 8, 2, 1
Hike 21 - Long Loop, 1, 2, 8-17, 9, 8, 2, 1
Hike 22 - West Maroon Pass, 1, 2, 8, 9, 17, 18, RETURN
Hike 23 - Aspen, 1, 2, 8, 9, 17-29, SHUTTLE

shuttle to Aspen parking lot

Maroon Lake
mile 9.94
9,575'
28

29

END
HIKE 23
mile 10.22
9,560'

junction
mile 8.55
10,120'
27

Crater Lake
mile 8.31
10,098'
26

view Crater Lake
mile 7.55   10,349'
25

talus slope
mile 7.1
10,379'
24

23 talus slope

22 cross creek: shoes
mile 6.72   10,502'

21 cross creek: shoes
mile 5.92   10,902'

20 cross creek: shoes
mile 4.76   11,650'

19 cross creek: shoes
mile 4.4   11,904'

18 West Maroon Pass
mile 3.91   12,484'

junction
11,702'
17

MILES
0   0.5   1

- 68 -

West Maroon to
17 Hasley Pass Loop

Hasley Pass

Distance	5.50-mile loop
Difficulty Rating	Moderate if hiked counterclockwise. More strenuous clockwise.
Surface	Mostly easy packed dirt to the pass; some loose rock on return route.
Gradient	Easy and moderate, with one steep section up and one down.
Average Time	3 hours, 30 minutes.
Elevations	TH: 10,417; Highest:12,121; Gain: +1,693
Maps	Latitude 40 Crested Butte, Taylor Park; Trails Illustrated 128. Trail 1970
Star Rating	☆☆☆☆☆☆

Highlights

In season, waist-high wildflowers smother the hillsides. From the summit, see Snowmass Peak. Its massive granite walls strike a contrast against the towering red peaks of the Ruby Range. Together, they completely encircle the basin in classic Colorado scenery. The return route is higher than the approach route, allowing expansive views of Mount Bellview, Treasury Mountain, Paradise Pass, and the West Maroon Valley.

> **Directions To Trailhead:** From CBVC, drive north 14.08 miles on Gothic Road CR 317. SUV recommended after mile 12. The road gets very narrow with high cliffs. Drive over Schofield Pass and down the other side to the marked trailhead and parking lot.

Trail Description

Many hikers miss this splendid hike in favor of the more famous West Maroon Pass. Yet, this hike is shorter and easier overall. The trail starts with a climb along the cascading Crystal River as it twists through spruce forest. By 0.53 miles, the river and forest are left behind, and the trail splits **2**. A sign indicates to go right to West Maroon Pass, but does not tell you about the left fork. That fork is your return route. For now, go right. The full glory of the seasonal wildflower meadows display their splendor as the trail meanders leisurely through a natural garden.

At mile 1.94 **9**, the trail forks again. The left (NW) fork leads to Hasley Pass. This moderately steep gradient persists until you reach an unnamed alpine basin at mile 2.65.

From the summit **11**, the views across Hasley Basin to Snowmass Peak are breathtaking. Hasley Basin is, in our opinion, the most stunning valley in the book. Turn around 180 degrees and see the entire West Maroon Valley to West Maroon Pass. Enjoy!

The trail meanders through wildflowers

When you descend from the pass, there is no obvious trail to show you where the return route goes **10** . Leave the trail you came up. Head south across the alpine basin. Stay parallel to the ridge that borders the western edge. It is a gentle descent to the end of the ridgeline. You should see a major trail where the terrain suddenly plummets over cliffs.

After a steep descent, the trail flattens out on a bench. It is easy to miss your turn south **3** . There is no sign. The visible trail continues west, then north, around the other side of the ridge. A shallow gully heading south is your clue. Follow it, staying high on its western edge. You will find the trail continuing from there. After this, the trail is easy to follow back to your vehicle. It is a marvelous route that few hikers know.

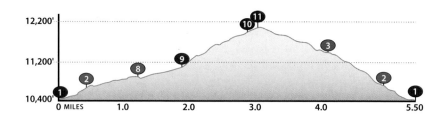

Return route

GPS	Mile	Latitude	Longitude	Elevation	Comment
1	0.0	39,1,29N	107,3,0W	10,417'	Start West Maroon to Hasley Pass Loop.
2	0.53	39,1,36N	107,2,38W	10,690'	Junction: return route from Hasley Pass. Go right.
8	1.31	39,1,57N	107,1,54W	10,908'	Unmarked junction: to Trail 401.
9	1.94	39,2,23N	107,1,27W	11,132'	Junction: Hasley Basin Trail. Go west.
10	2.95	39,2,41N	107,2,15W	11,992'	Junction: return route. No trail.
11	3.15	39,2,48N	107,2,18W	12,121'	Hasley Pass.
10	3.35	39,2,41N	107,2,1W	11,992'	Junction: no trail. Go south along base of western ridge.
3	4.24	39,2,8N	107,2,25W	11,511'	Junction: go south to find trail.
2	5.06	39,1,36N	107,2,38W	10,690'	Junction: rejoin main West Maroon Trail.
1	5.50	39,1,29N	107,3,0W	10,417'	Finish Hasley Pass Loop.

Return route views of valley

West Maroon to Crystal
(shuttle or Out & Back)

Hiking out bench

Distance	6.7 miles from start to shuttle point
Difficulty Rating	Moderate with 2 difficult sections.
Surface	Easy packed dirt.
Gradient	Difficult uphill to bench. Easy across bench. Steep downhill to Crystal Road.
Average Time	4 hours, 30 minutes.
Elevations	TH: 10,417; Highest: 11,521; Gain: +1,466 Loss: -2,687 feet.
Maps	Latitude 40 Crested Butte, Taylor Park. Trail 1970 to no number.
Star Rating	☆☆☆☆☆☆☆

Highlights

Cross easy benchland for 3 miles, taking in unparalleled views of Mount Bellview, Cinnamon Mountain, Mount Baldy, Treasury Mountain, Galena Lake, Crystal Peak, Whitehouse Mountain, and so much more. An old route that is hardly used.

> **Directions To Trailhead:** From CBVC, drive north 14.08 miles on Gothic Road CR 317. SUV recommended after mile 12. The road gets very narrow with high cliffs. Drive over Schofield Pass and down the other side to the marked trail-head and parking lot.

> **Shuttle:** This is a difficult shuttle. It is only 4 miles back to the trailhead, but the 4x4 road above Crystal is the famous Devil's Punchbowl route, which is extreme. To hike all the way back would turn an easy day into a strenuous one. If you cannot arrange a shuttle with a jeep or ATV, we recommend hiking the bench to **5**, then returning.

Trail Description

This is a route very few hikers know. Read the description for hike 17 to **2**. At the junction, go left. The climb up to the bench is steep. The open meadows, filled with seasonal wildflowers, allow for expansive views of Mount Bellview and Paradise Pass. The trail fades as you approach the bench. Bear left (NW), and you will find it **3**.

Treasury Mountain consumes the horizon. Peer down into the Devil's Punchbowl. See the majestic peaks of the Elk Mountains in the Lead King Basin area. The trail is easy packed dirt. You may not meet any other hikers. This is a superb outing.

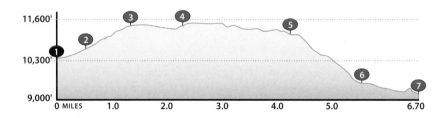

Belleview Mountain

Hikers have made the circuit to Crystal and hiked back through Devil's Punchbowl to the trailhead. To do this, add 4 miles distance and 1,696 feet elevation gain to this description. Then be mindful that the trail back is rocky to the extreme. If you prefer to keep the day easy, turn around before the trail starts the steep descent to the Crystal River. That would make your turnaround point at or before .5 , which is 4.36 miles from the start. Above all, do not dismiss this hike because you don't have a shuttle. It is a marvelous out and back trek, no matter the distance.

Crystal Gorge

Treasury Mountain

GPS	Mile	Latitude	Longitude	Elevation	Comment
1	0.0	39,1,29N	107,3,0W	10,417'	Start West Maroon to Crystal.
2	0.53	39,1,36N	107,2,38W	10,690'	Unmarked junction: turn left (N).
3	1.37	39,2,8N	107,2,25W	11,511'	Junction: to Hasley Pass. Go left (NW).
4	2.35	39,2,45N	107,3,3W	11,521'	Trail splits high & low. Either trail is okay.
5	4.36	39,3,56N	107,4,8W	11,191'	Cross creek. Trail descends steeply from here. If you do not have a shuttle, we recommend turning back.
6	5.68	39,4,20N	107,5,18W	9,556'	Junction: trail meets 4x4 road from Lead King Basin to Crystal. Turn left (south).
7	6.70	39,3,36N	107,5,49W	9,167'	Finish. Junction: 4x4 road to Crystal & Schofield Pass. Turn left (SE) if hiking out. Otherwise, meet shuttle here.

West Maroon to Frigid Air Pass

View from Frigid Air Pass

Distance	9.28 miles out & back.
Difficulty Rating	Moderate.
Surface	Mostly easy packed dirt with just a few sections of rocky terrain.
Gradient	Mostly easy to moderate. Very steep (225 feet in 0.15 miles) to Frigid Air Pass.
Average Time	6 hours.
Elevations	TH: 10,417; Highest: 12,401; Gain: +2,104
Maps	Latitude 40 Crested Butte, Taylor Park; Trails Illustrated # 128 . Trail 1970
Star Rating	☆☆☆☆☆☆☆

Highlights

This is a hike of superlatives. The wildflower meadows from mid-July to mid-August display an astonishing variety of species and color. The valley climbs up and up, hugging the numerous peaks in flowers and greenery. The entire hike is open to vistas.

> **Directions To Trailhead:** From CBVC, drive north 14.08 miles on Gothic Road CR 317. SUV recommended after mile 12. The road gets very narrow with high cliffs. Drive over Schofield Pass and down the other side to the marked trailhead and parking lot.

Trail Description

Another unforgettable hike begins at the West Maroon Trailhead. Hike up the easy trail to the Hasley Pass junction **9**. This section is almost entirely through seasonally flower festooned hillsides of amazing color and variety. After the junction, the trail turns northeasterly, cutting through more waist high wildflowers. As it ascends, look behind to see snow capped Treasury Mountain appear.

At the next signed junction **17**, begin the railroad grade ascent towards Frigid Air Pass. As the trail contours through the mid-section of Belleview Mountain, you have an eagle's eye view of the entire valley. From **16**, ascend the steep and strenuous 0.21-mile trail to the summit **15**, where you can enjoy a close-up view of the Maroon Bells and down into the green meadows of Fravert Basin. To the southwest, across Hasley Pass, stands the Ruby Range, Yule Pass, Cinnamon Mountain, and Treasury Mountain. In mid-July, these peaks were glistening white with snow. Look north and you can see West Maroon Pass. All in all, an incredible day of hiking surrounded by outstanding scenery.

Treasury Mountain appears

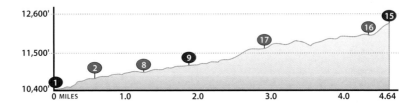

Junction to West Maroon Pass

Down valley views after junction

GPS	Mile	Latitude	Longitude	Elevation	Comment
1	0.0	39,1,29N	107,3,0W	10,417'	Start West Maroon to Frigid Air Pass.
2	0.53	39,1,36N	107,2,38W	10,690'	Junction: to Crystal & Hasley Pass.
8	1.31	39,1,57N	107,1,54W	10,908'	Unmarked junction: to Trail 401.
9	1.94	39,2,23N	107,1,27W	11,132'	Junction: Hasley Basin Trail.
17	3.0	39,2,18N	107,0,32W	11,702'	Junction: to West Maroon Pass.
16	4.43	39,3,8N	107,1,26W	12,040'	Junction: to Hasley Basin.
15	4.64	39,3,13N	107,1,12W	12,401'	Frigid Air Pass.

West Maroon
Short Loop

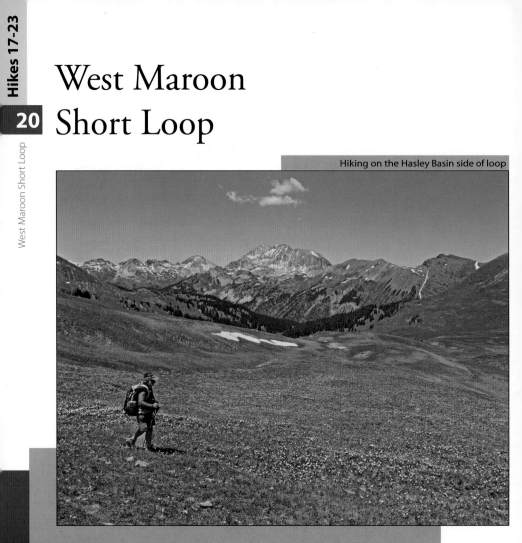

Hiking on the Hasley Basin side of loop

Distance	9.43-mile loop.
Difficulty Rating	Moderate.
Surface	Mostly easy packed dirt.
Gradient	Mostly easy and moderate, with two difficult sections.
Average Time	6 hours, 30 minutes.
Elevations	TH: 10,417; Highest: 12,401; Gain: +2,306
Maps	Latitude 40 Crested Butte, Taylor Park; Trails Illustrated # 128. Trail 1970.
Star Rating	☆☆☆☆☆☆

Highlights

This hike combines the beauty and diversity of Hasley Pass and Frigid Air Pass into one loop. What makes this loop so special is the time spent contouring around the Hasley Basin side, with its views of Snowmass Mountain and the Ruby Range.

> Directions To Trailhead: From CBVC, drive north 14.08 miles on Gothic Road CR 317. SUV recommended after mile 12. The road gets very narrow with high cliffs. Drive over Schofield Pass and down the other side to the marked trailhead and parking lot.

Trail Description

Hasley Pass and Frigid Air Pass are superb hikes by themselves, and each by itself is shorter in distance than the loop described here. Yet, this trail offers an opportunity to hike a lesser known, short, off-trail section with vistas unseen from the West Maroon side.

Read the description for hike 18 to **11** . Standing at the pass, looking at Snowmass Mountain to the north, there are two rounded knobs due east of your view. Your goal is to hike around these knobs on the Hasley Basin side, which is to the northwest.

From the summit, take the trail leading to Hasley Basin's valley floor about 0.3 miles downhill. A large talus slope cascades down the northwest side of the first knob. Look for a faint trail across this slide **12**. Hike across the slide. On the other side, the trail leads down into Hasley Basin again. Leave the trail and turn east. Walk off trail and contour past the second knob. There are possible trails fading in and out. Your goal is to reach the ridgeline ahead that runs in a northwest-southeast direction.

When you make the easy trek to this last ridgeline, you will see an old Forest

Heading for Frigid Air Pass

Service sign. From this sign, follow the direction for Fravert Basin. You have a clear view of the steep trail to Frigid Air Pass. Ascend the strenuous trail to the summit **15**, where you can enjoy a close-up view of the Maroon Bells and down into the green meadows of Fravert Basin. To the southwest stand the Ruby Range, Yule Pass, Cinnamon Mountain, and Treasury Mountain. In mid-July, these peaks were glistening white with snow.

Once off the high summit, the trail contours through the mid-section of Belleview Mountain, giving you views of the entire West Maroon Valley. From the junction with West Maroon Pass **17**, it is 3.03 miles to the trailhead. It is all downhill, through waist high wildflowers, mountains all around. What a glorious day this has been!

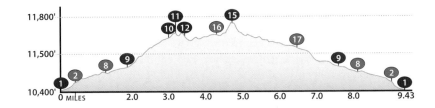

Down valley view of Treasury Mountain

Descending Frigid Air Pass

GPS	Mile	Latitude	Longitude	Elevation	Comment
1	0.0	39,1,29N	107,3,0W	10,417'	Start West Maroon Short Loop.
2	0.53	39,1,36N	107,2,38W	10,690'	Junction: stay on main trail.
8	1.31	39,1,57N	107,1,54W	10,908'	Unmarked junction: to Trail 401.
9	1.94	39,2,23N	107,1,27W	11,132'	Junction: Hasley Basin Trail. Go left (NW).
10	2.95	39,2,41N	107,2,1W	11,992'	Unmarked junction for Hasley Loop. Stay on trail
11	3.15	39,2,48N	107,2,18W	12,121'	Hasley Pass.
12	3.46	39,2,59N	107,2,12W	11,985'	Leave trail. Turn right (NE) and cross talus.
16	4.37	39,3,8N	107,1,26W	12,040'	Junction: go left (N) to Frigid Air Pass.
15	4.73	39,3,13N	107,1,12W	12,401'	Frigid Air Pass.
16	5.09	39,3,8N	107,1,26W	12,040'	Junction: go left (SE)
17	6.40	39,2,18N	107,0,32W	11,702'	Junction: go right (NW).
9	7.53	39,2,23N	107,1,27W	11,132'	Junction: Hasley Basin Trail.
8	8.18	39,1,57N	107,1,54W	10,908'	Unmarked junction: to Trail 401.
2	8.96	39,1,36N	107,2,38W	10,690'	Junction: stay on main trail.
1	9.43	39,1,29N	107,3,0W	10,417'	Finish West Maroon Short Loop.

West Maroon

21 # Long Loop

Distance	14.2-mile loop.
Difficulty Rating	Difficult due to distance and elevation gain.
Surface	Easy packed dirt.
Gradient	Mostly moderate with three steep sections.
Average Time	10 hours.
Elevations	TH:10,417; Highest: 12,401; Gain: +3,752
Maps	Latitude 40 Crested Butte, Taylor Park. Trail 1970
Star Rating	

Hasley Pass Views down valley

Highlights

A classic Colorado wilderness hike over two passes and through incredibly picturesque valleys. Vast views, cliffs, rivers, basins, waterfalls—this hike has it all. Wildflowers and aspens offer astounding colors in season.

Directions To Trailhead: From CBVC, drive north 14.08 miles on Gothic Road CR 317. SUV recommended after mile 12. The road gets very narrow with high cliffs. Drive over Schofield Pass and down the other side to the marked trailhead and parking lot.

Trail Description

This is one of the most difficult but most rewarding hikes in the area. The elevation gain is over 3,700 feet. Even though there are many downhill sections, and much of the climbing is spread out over long distances, by the time you climb from Fravert Basin to the top of Frigid Air Pass you may have sapped the remainder of your energy unless you are adequately prepared.

Read the directions for hike 17 to **11**. From the top of Hasley Pass, follow the trail north, down into the basin of open meadows blooming with seasonal wildflowers. Hasley Basin is a treasure and offers the hearty hiker solitude and remote wilderness.

The last 0.50 miles to junction **13** , the trail enters a forested area. After this junction, the trail passes through alternating forest and meadows until just before starting the climb up to Frigid Air Pass, at which point there is a beautiful waterfall and beaver ponds **14** .

After the ponds, the trail climbs steeply for 0.3 miles. During this climb, you are exposed to some of the most unique scenery in the area, with cascading water falls at your feet and the beaver ponds below. Enter an upper valley that feels devoid of human influence. The trail moves between forest and meadow. After some time, you break out into the open and can see the route up to Frigid Air Pass. You have entered Fravert Basin.

Here may be the crux. At this point, the remainder of the hike to the top may be exhausting if you are not in good condition. The climb is moderate, but sustained. Once you have reached the Frigid Air summit **15** , it is still another 4.62 miles to the finish. Although it is downhill, and the views of West Maroon Valley are teeming with photo ops, it is quite a distance to accomplish after what you have already done.

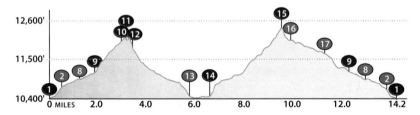

GPS	Mile	Latitude	Longitude	Elevation	Comment
1	0.0	39,1,29N	107,3,0W	10,417'	Start West Maroon Long Loop.
2	0.53	39,1,36N	107,2,38W	10,690'	Junction: to Crystal & Hasley Pass.
8	1.31	39,1,57N	107,1,54W	10,908'	Unmarked junction: to Trail 401.
9	1.94	39,2,23N	107,1,27W	11,132'	Junction: to Hasley Pass.
10	2.95	39,2,41N	107,2,1W	11,992'	Unmarked junction for Hasley Loop. No trail.
11	3.15	39,2,48N	107,2,18W	12,121'	Hasley Pass.
12	3.46	39,2,59N	107,2,12W	11,985'	Junction: faint trail across talus. Continue on main trail heading downhill (north).
13	5.84	39,4,57N	107,2,28W	10,455'	Junction: to Frigid Air Pass. Turn right (East).
14	6.46	39,4,47N	107,1,50W	10,487'	Ponds and waterfall.
15	9.58	39,3,13N	107,1,12W	12,401'	Frigid Air Pass.
16	9.94	39,3,8N	107,1,26W	12,040'	Junction: go left (southeast)
17	11.19	39,2,18N	107,0,32W	11,702'	Junction: go right (north).
9	12.3	39,2,23N	107,1,27W	11,132'	Junction: to Hasley Pass.
8	12.95	39,1,57N	107,1,54W	10,908	Unmarked junction: to Trail 401.
2	13.73	39,1,36N	107,2,38W	10,690'	Junction: to Crystal & Hasley Pass.
1	14.2	39,1,29N	107,3,0W	10,417'	Finish West Maroon Long Loop.

Fravert Basin

Hiking in Hasley Basin

Start ascent to Fravert Basin

West Maroon to West Maroon Pass

Distance	7.82 miles out & back.
Difficulty Rating	Moderate with difficult climb last 0.25 miles.
Surface	Mostly easy packed dirt with just a few sections of rocky terrain.
Gradient	Mostly easy to moderate. Very steep last 0.25 miles to West Maroon Pass.
Average Time	5 hours.
Elevations	TH: 10,417; Highest: 12,484; Gain: +2,040
Maps	Latitude 40 Crested Butte, Taylor Park; Trails Illustrated #128. Trail 1970
Star Rating	

West Maroon Pass

Highlights

In season, wildflowers spread like carpets across the fertile hillsides. The higher the trail ascends, the thicker they grow, with different species and colors mixing together. From the craggy summit, the views off both sides are nothing short of awesome.

Directions To Trailhead: From CBVC, drive north 14.08 miles on Gothic Road CR 317. SUV recommended after mile 12. The road gets very narrow with high cliffs. Drive over Schofield Pass and down the other side to the marked trailhead and parking lot.

Trail Description

This is perhaps the most popular of the West Maroon trails. Though in our opinion Hasley Pass and Frigid Air Pass are equal in splendor, folks who have time for only one hike seem to choose this one. On weekends, the trail may be as colorful with hikers as with flowers.

The 3 mile hike to Frigid Air junction **17** is a stroll through seasonal wildflower hillsides. The valley opens wider as you ascend, offering views of surrounding peaks.

From the signed junction where the trail forks left to Frigid Air Pass **18** , you can see up valley to the sharp rock pinnacles that mark West Maroon Pass. Treasury Mountain, still snow-covered at the end of July, is framed by thick purple, yellow, and blue fields of flowers. You can spot the route to Hasley Pass, and see the notch for Frigid Air Pass, all from this vantage point.

As you hike up from this junction, the trail gets a little steeper step by step. At 11,702 feet, you have another 782 feet to climb in 0.89 miles. Soon, you will summit a small knoll

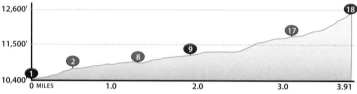

Final ascent to pass

where a creek spreads out to water a small basin of alpine flowers. Framed with the down valley views, it makes for a beautiful photograph. After crossing this, the trail begins the strenuous final ascent to the pass. When you reach the summit **18** , you can see forever in all directions. It is a small summit, crammed with rock pinnacles and dropping steeply off both sides. What a spot for a well deserved rest.

View from small basin with creek

Treasury Mountain and fields of flowers

GPS	Mile	Latitude	Longitude	Elevation	Comment
1	0.0	39,1,29N	107,3,0W	10,417'	Start West Maroon to West Maroon Pass.
2	0.53	39,1,36N	107,2,38W	10,690'	Junction: to Crystal & Hasley Pass.
8	1.31	39,1,57N	107,1,54W	10,908'	Unmarked junction: to Trail 401.
9	1.94	39,2,23N	107,1,27W	11,132'	Junction: Hasley Basin Trail. Go right (N).
17	3.0	39,2,18N	107,0,32W	11,702'	Junction: to Frigid Air Pass. Go East.
18	3.91	39,2,10N	106,59,51W	12,484'	West Maroon Pass.

West Maroon to Aspen

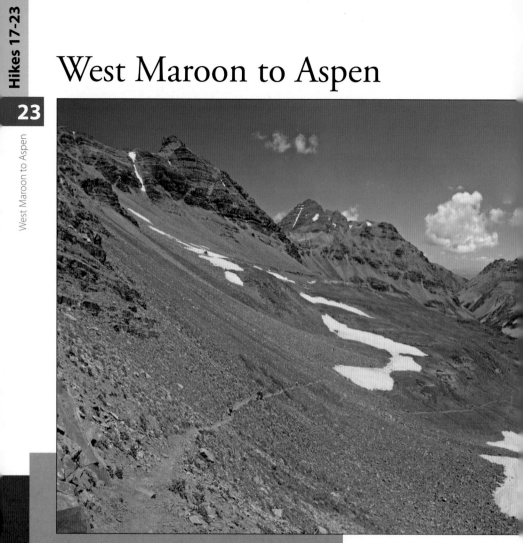

Distance	10.22 miles.
	(River crossing shoes recommended).
Difficulty Rating	Mostly moderate with a difficult 0.25-mile climb to West Maroon Pass.
Surface	Mostly easy packed dirt on West Maroon side. Mostly very rocky on Aspen side.
Gradient	Easy & moderate. Very steep last 0.25 miles to West Maroon Pass.
Average Time	7 hours.
Elevations	TH: 10,417; Highest: 12,484; Gain:+2,180; Loss: -3,032
Maps	Trails Illustrated # 128. Trail 1970.
Star Rating	☆☆☆☆☆

View of Aspen side from pass

Highlights

In season, wildflowers spread like carpets across the fertile hillsides. The higher the trail ascends, the thicker they grow, with different species and colors mixing together. From the craggy summit, the views off both sides are nothing short of awesome.

Directions To Trailhead: From CBVC, drive north 14.08 miles on Gothic Road CR 317. SUV recommended after mile 12. The road gets very narrow with high cliffs. Drive over Schofield Pass and down the other side to the marked trailhead and parking lot.

Shuttle: Many folks spend the night in Aspen and hike back the following day.

Trail Description

This is the most famous of the West Maroon Trails. On good weather days, there may be as many as 20 to 30 people hiking this route from one side or the other.

Follow the description for hike 22 to West Maroon Pass. The view from the top of **18** looking towards Aspen encompasses Belleview Mountain, whose flank the trail descends, all the way down the Elk Range to Sievers Mountain. To the east, Pyramid Peak spreads its long ridges north and south, embracing the entire Maroon Creek Valley. All together, they form an impressive visual and physical barrier that funnels the trail down the valley squeezed between.

The trail descending to Aspen starts out very steep and narrow, with areas of slippery side hill. The gradient gradually gets easier as elevation is lost, but most all of the trail, all the way to Maroon Lake, is very rocky. This, in our opinion, adds a measure of difficulty not encountered on the Crested Butte side.

The valley stays open to views of the surrounding mountains until mile 5.92 **21** , where it narrows considerably, while high brush and spruce forest tend to limit views to occasional openings. There are three crossings of Maroon Creek (wet shoes recommended). By mile 6.9 **23** , the flanks of the Maroon Bells have squeezed the valley even tighter. Numerous talus slopes stretch across the valley floor. After crossing the last slope **25** , you look down on Crater Lake and the more open valley in which it rests.

From Crater Lake, it is 1.89 miles to the trailhead. The rocky surface has given no quarter, however, remaining faithful to its character to the end. Only

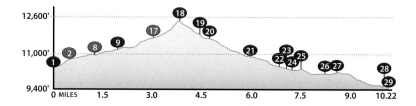

View of Crater Lake

the last 0.25 miles follows an easy gravel path designed for the thousands of tourists who visit Maroon Lake. This lake view is one of the most photographed places in the world.

At the present time, the free bus on the Aspen side stops service at 5:00 pm. If you have missed this last bus, you could hitch a ride. There may be other late hikers doing the same. The Aspen Chamber of Commerce can help arrange lodging. If you plan to hike back to Crested Butte, the ascent from Aspen to West Maroon Pass is 7 miles with 2,924 elevation gain. From Crested Butte, you hiked 4 miles with 2,067 feet of gain.

Descending West Maroon Pass to Aspen

Backpackers ascend from the Aspen side.

GPS	Mile	Latitude	Longitude	Elevation	Comment
1	0.0	39,1,29N	107,3,0W	10,417′	Start West Maroon to Aspen.
2	0.53	39,1,36N	107,2,38W	10,690′	Junction: to Crystal & Hasley Pass.
8	1.31	39,1,57N	107,1,54W	10,908′	Unmarked junction: to Trail 401.
9	1.94	39,2,23N	107,1,27W	11,132′	Junction: Hasley Basin Trail. Go right (N).
17	3.0	39,2,18N	107,0,32W	11,702′	Junction: to West Maroon Pass. Go east.
18	3.91	39,2,10N	106,59,51W	12,484′	Summit West Maroon Pass.
19	4.40	39,2,23N	106,59,30W	11,904′	Cross Maroon Creek.
20	4.76	39,2,32N	106,59,16W	11,650′	Cross tributary creek.
21	5.92	39,3,19N	106,58,37W	10,902′	Cross Maroon Creek. Shoes or poles.
22	6.72	39,3,55N	106,58,17W	10,502′	Cross Maroon Creek. Rock bridge.
23	6.90	39,4,4N	106,58,14W	10,444′	Talus slopes begin.
24	7.10	39,4,14N	106,58,14W	10,379′	Second talus slope.
25	7.55	39,4,36N	106,58,21W	10,349′	End talus slopes. View Crater Lake.
26	8.31	39,5,11N	106,58,5W	10,098′	Lakeshore.
27	8.55	39,5,20N	106,57,58W	10,120′	Junction: Maroon-Snowmass Trail 1975.
28	9.94	39,5,53N	106,56,46W	9,575′	Junction: Crater Lake Trail & View Trail.
29	10.22	39,5,55N	106,56,28W	9,560′	End West Maroon to Aspen.

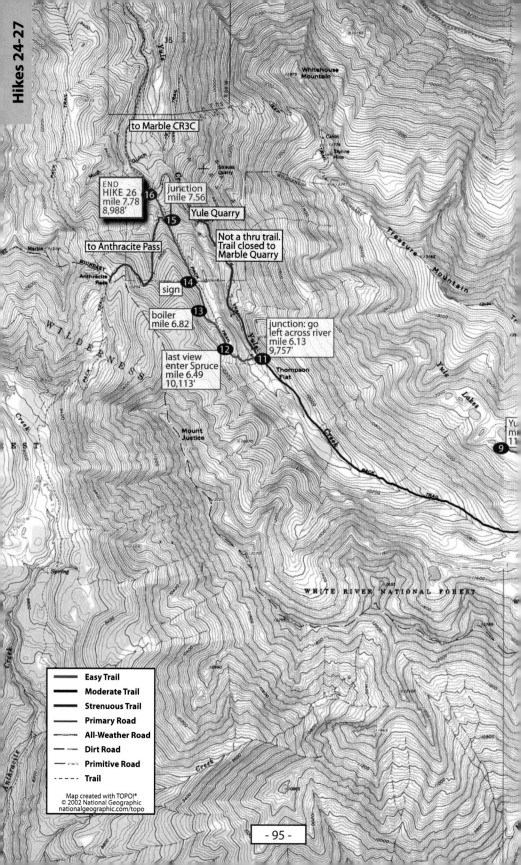

to Marble CR3C

END
HIKE 26
mile 7.78
8,988'

16

junction
mile 7.56

Yule Quarry

15

Not a thru trail.
Trail closed to
Marble Quarry

to Anthracite Pass

sign

14

boiler
mile 6.82

13

junction: go
left across river
mile 6.13
9,757'

12

last view
enter Spruce
mile 6.49
10,113'

11

Thompson
Flat

Mount
Justice

Whitehouse
Mountain

Treasure Mountain

Yule Lakes

Yu
mi
11

9

WHITE RIVER NATIONAL FOREST

	Easy Trail
	Moderate Trail
	Strenuous Trail
	Primary Road
	All-Weather Road
	Dirt Road
	Primitive Road
	Trail

Map created with TOPO!®
© 2002 National Geographic
nationalgeographic.com/topo

FOLLOW THE GPS POINTS

Hike 24 - Paradise Pass to Yule Pass, 1-2, RETURN

Hike 25 - Paradise Pass to Yule Lakes, 1-9, RETURN

Hike 26 - Paradise Pass to Marble Pass, 1-3, 10-16, SHUTTLE

Hike 27 - Paradise Pass to Cinnamon, 1, 12-21, RETURN

creek
mile 3.19

dead end

junction
mile 2.7

dead end

END HIKE 24
Yule Pass
mile 2.1
11,702'

Cinnamon
12,286'

to Schofield Pass
easiest road to Crested Butte

WHITE RIVER
CR 734

Cinnamon
Mtn.

**START
HIKES 24–27**
Paradise Basin Trails
11,315'

Paradise
Basin

Slate River
Road CR 734

very narrow, steep road
to Crested Butte

MILES
0   0.5   1

Paradise Pass to Yule Pass

Distance	4.2 miles out & back.
Difficulty Rating	Easy.
Surface	Broken rock and talus all the way. Very narrow with cliffs half the route.
Gradient	Easy.
Average Time	2 hours, 30 minutes.
Elevations	TH: 11,315; Highest: 11,702; Gain: +495
Maps	40 Crested Butte, Taylor Park. Trail 576
Star Rating	

View across the river canyon

Highlights

A very short hike, with an easy railroad grade and panoramic mountain and valley vistas from start to finish. Peer straight down into the steep, deep Slate River Gorge as it carves its way to Crested Butte. Cascading waterfalls thunder down precipitous cliffs. This is raw land, constantly changing by force of wind and water.

Directions To Trailhead: From CBVC, drive north 13.37 miles on Gothic Road CR 317 to Schofield Pass. SUVs recommended beyond mile 12. The road gets very narrow with high cliffs. Just past Schofield Pass, turn left (SW) on CR 734 to Paradise Basin. Drive 2.3 miles to Paradise Pass. Turn right (W) at Yule Pass sign. There are three roads. Turn right, (NE) and drive 0.2 miles further to a parking area. Hike west up the old mining road. There is a trailhead sign ahead.

Trail Description

To find a short trail with an easy gradient in the Colorado Rockies is a bit of a miracle. This old mining road transported goods to Marble. Beware, however, as much of the road has washed away, leaving narrow passage across numerous sections. The bare rock slopes drop away one thousand feet. If you are afraid of heights, or fear walking beside steep cliffs, you may not want to walk this trail. Hikers must also be patient and wait for winter snows to melt. Very dangerous snow slopes may cover the trail until late July.

Barring the above conditions, this trail is nothing short of spectacular. It hangs on the rocky flank of Cinnamon Mountain, while the Slate River, just barely born, carves deeply down 1,000 feet through the soft, bare rock. Cinnamon Mountain, Purple Mountain, and Treasury Mountain all rise straight up. It is 3,000 vertical feet from mountain top to river bottom, and this trail cuts right through the mid-section.

Once at the summit **2**, there are three trails evident, and no signs. The left trail provides access to summiting Purple Mountain, a very technical ascent. The center trail gives access to Yule Lakes and the town of Marble. These are described in hikes 25 and 26. The right-hand trail provides access to Treasury Mountain. If you don't wish to pursue one of these additional treks, make the summit your turnaround point. It has already been a marvelous day hike.

View towards Paradise Pass

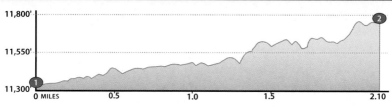

View towards Marble from pass

GPS	Mile	Latitude	Longitude	Elevation	Comment
1	0.0	38,59,28N	107,3,57W	11,315'	Start Paradise Pass to Yule Pass.
2	2.10	39,0,2N	107,5,53W	11,702'	Yule Pass summit. Turnaround.

View of Yule Pass from narrow part of trail

Paradise Pass to Yule Lakes

Distance	8.2 miles out & back.
Difficulty Rating	Easy to Yule Pass; moderate to mile 2.7; difficult to Lakes.
Surface	Mixture of very rocky, broken talus, alpine tundra, and slab rock.
Gradient	Easy to Yule Pass; moderate to mile 2.7; steep to Lakes.
Average Time	7 hours.
Elevations	TH: 11,315; Highest: 11,983; Gain: +1,203; Loss: -673
Maps	Latitude 40 Crested Butte, Taylor Park. Trail 576 to 2083 then off-trail.
Star Rating	✩✩✩✩✩✩✩

First Yule Lake

Highlights

Pristine mountain lakes at the base of Treasury Mountain. There is no trail plotted on any map, so these lakes receive few visitors. This is a route finding experience through rugged alpine scenery.

Directions To Trailhead: From CBVC, drive north 13.37 miles on Gothic Road CR 317 to Schofield Pass. SUVs recommended beyond mile 12. The road gets very narrow with high cliffs. Just past Schofield Pass, turn left (SW) on CR 734 to Paradise Basin. Drive 2.3 miles to Paradise Pass. Turn right (W) at Yule Pass sign. There are three roads. Turn right, (NE) and drive 0.2 miles further to a parking area. Hike west up the old mining road. There is a trailhead sign ahead.

Trail is faint.

Trail Description

Read the description for hike 24 to ②. From the summit of Yule Pass, take the middle trail that goes down valley for 0.7 miles to an unmarked junction ③. Go right (N). Look down valley and locate the long, red rock ridgeline stemming north to south off Treasury Mountain. If you follow the ridgeline down, you will see a saddle at the far southern end. Yule Lake is immediately on the other side of this saddle. Your goal is to hike towards a point above the saddle. Keep this in mind, as the trail becomes very faint about halfway there.

The north-heading trail is steep. The beautiful Yule Valley below unfolds as you climb. After reaching a first bench ④, climb again to another. The trail is easy to

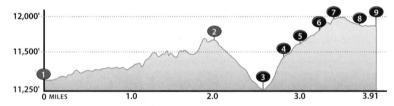

Route to Yule Lake from junction

SADDLE

follow, until it crosses a stream verdant with wildflowers and enclosed by low granite walls **5**. It is easy to lose sight of any trail after crossing this stream. Head west, keeping a contour that gains elevation slowly. Look for the red ridgeline and the saddle. You cannot go too low because of cliffs, and you will not want to climb too high due to steepness. The terrain is rugged, and tiring. You should find the path again if you pass remnants of digging pits **6**. Soon a long gully leading from the valley floor up to the saddle becomes evident. It is best to stay above the red rock cliffs that border this gully and approach the saddle **8** from above. The trail becomes well defined again through this area. You cannot see the lake until you are over the top of the saddle. Then, suddenly, you are there. What a hike!

After crossing creek, trail is faint

GPS	Mile	Latitude	Longitude	Elevation	Comment
1	0.0	38,59,28N	107,3,57W	11,315'	Start Paradise Pass to Yule Lakes.
2	2.1	39,0,2N	107,5,53W	11,702'	Yule Pass summit. Take middle path.
3	2.7	39,0,17N	107,6,24W	11,281'	Junction: go right (N) to Yule Lakes.
4	2.96	39,0,29N	107,6,25W	11,570'	Reach the first bench.
5	3.19	39,0,34N	107,6,36W	11,766'	Cross creek. Trail is faint. Hike west.
6	3.42	39,0,38N	107,6,49W	11,846'	Old digging pit. Trail improves again.
7	3.64	39,0,43N	107,7,4W	11,983'	Highest elevation point.
8	3.90	39,0,42N	107,7,19W	11,900'	Saddle.
9	4.1	39,0,45N	107,7,31W	11,847'	Yule Lake.

Narrow trail to Yule Pass

Paradise Pass to Marble (shuttle)

To Beaver Ponds (Out & Back)

View of Yule Valley with beaver ponds below

Distance	7.78 miles to shuttle (Marble); 7.12 miles out & back (Ponds).
Difficulty Rating	Moderate.
Surface	Talus to Yule Pass. Easy packed dirt with few rocky sections to Marble.
Gradient	Very easy to Yule Pass. Moderate descent to Ponds & Thompson Flat. Steep ascent and descent from flats to Marble trailhead.
Average Time	5 hours to Marble.
Elevations	TH: 11,315; Highest: 11,702; Gain: +974 or +495; Loss: -3,296 or -763
Maps	Latitude 40 Crested Butte, Taylor Park. Trail 576 to 2083
Star Rating	

Highlights

This hike has panoramic mountain and valley vistas from the trailhead all the way to the last mile to Marble Quarry Road. The Yule Valley is a gem of luxuriant meadows pierced by the meandering Yule Creek. Beaver ponds, waterfalls, dramatic cliffs, and sharp peaks create an unparalleled wilderness hike.

Directions To Trailhead: From CBVC, drive north 13.37 miles on Gothic Road CR 317 to Schofield Pass. SUVs recommended beyond mile 12. The road gets very narrow with high cliffs. Just past Schofield Pass, turn left (SW) on CR 734 to Paradise Basin. Drive 2.3 miles to Paradise Pass. Turn right (W) at Yule Pass sign. There are three roads. Turn right, (NE) and drive 0.2 miles further to a parking area. Hike west up the old mining road. There is a trailhead sign ahead.

Shuttle: This is a long shuttle of about 62 miles one way from CBVC. Drive 59 miles to Marble via Kebler and McClure Passes. At the first stop sign in Marble, turn right (S). This is the gravel quarry road. Drive 2.85 miles and look for a 3-inch wide metal Forest Service sign that designates users. It is on a big switchback, just after a large pulloff area where landslides have decimated the drainage. There is parking for three cars just past the sign. If you have arrived at the quarry parking area, you have gone too far.

Trail Description

Read the description for hike 24 to **2**. From the summit of Yule Pass, the trail descends 3,296 feet to Marble. The verdant valley is wide and inviting, with Yule Creek flowing peacefully down the center. Since very few hikers bother to make the shuttle, the valley feels wild and untouched by human influence. Even if you descend only as far as the beaver ponds **10** and return the way you came, this section of the hike feels remote.

Start descending from Yule Pass to Marble

After the beaver ponds, the trail descends more seriously. It twists through small patches of spruce, following the creek as it tumbles along. As you approach Thompson Flat, the valley narrows severely. The easy trail, following the creek through the gorge on the right, is closed with barricades at the Marble Quarry. Hikers are prohibited passage. It is not closed, however, in Thompson Flat. Unaware hikers have certainly gone down the gorge only to have to return. A junction **11**, marked clearly on maps, is barley noticeable in reality. Very near the start of the gorge, keep looking for a prominent trail to the left (W) that crosses the river. You may need crossing shoes, even in October. After crossing, the trail ascends steeply (363 feet in 0.3 miles) up a mountainous bulge. Enjoy the vista at the top **12**. The trail enters dense spruce for the last mile.

Some hikers stay in Marble and hike back the next day. The historic Beaver Lake Lodge & Cabins has varied accommodations ranging from $79 to $109 for two at the time of this writing (www.beaverlakelodge.com). There is one restaurant with fantastic BBQ, but they are only open Thursday through Sunday. Best to check on this information. Remember, Marble is 2.85 miles down the quarry road from the trailhead. Traffic is minimal. Upgrade the return trip from moderate to difficult because of the elevation gain.

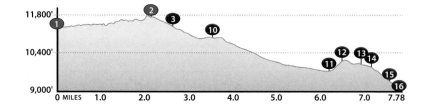

Route to Yule Pass

From Thompson Flat looking back

Route up mountainside

GPS	Mile	Latitude	Longitude	Elevation	Comment
1	0.0	38,59,28N	107,3,57W	11,315'	Start Yule Pass to Marble.
2	2.20	39,0,2N	107,5,53W	11,702'	Yule Pass summit. Take middle path.
3	2.70	39,0,17N	107,6,24W	11,281'	Junction: go straight ahead (W).
10	3.56	39,0,17N	107,7,13W	10,969'	Beaver ponds. Good turnaround for out & back.
11	6.13	39,1,17N	107,9,34W	9,757'	Unmarked junction: go left (W). Cross river.
12	6.49	39,1,22N	107,9,48W	10,133'	Top of climb. Enter spruce to finish.
13	6.82	39,1,36N	107,10,1W	9,946'	Boiler.
14	7.05	39,1,47N	107,10,6W	9,895'	Wilderness boundary sign.
15	7.56	39,2,10N	107,10,20W	9,309'	Junction: to Anthracite Pass.
16	7.78	39,2,20N	107,10,26W	8,988'	Finish on road to Marble Quarry CR 3C.

Paradise Pass to
27 Cinnamon Mountain

View from Cinnamon Mountain

Distance	2 miles out & back.
Difficulty Rating	Difficult.
Surface	Alpine tundra and broken talus.
Gradient	Moderate to very steep.
Average Time	2 hours, 30 minutes.
Elevations	TH: 11,315; Highest: 12,286; Gain: +964
Maps	LLatitude 40 Crested Butte, Taylor Park. No trails on any maps.
Star Rating	☆☆☆☆☆☆☆

Highlights

Wonderful views of the Maroon Bells, West Maroon Valley, Slate River Valley, Gunsight Pass, Crested Butte, Mount Baldy, Treasury Mountain, Yule Pass, and so much more. This peak makes you feel like you are soaring in a glider above all the wilderness west.

> **Directions To Trailhead:** From CBVC, drive north 13.37 miles on Gothic Road CR 317 to Schofield Pass. SUVs recommended beyond mile 12. The road gets very narrow with high cliffs. Just past Schofield Pass, turn left (SW) on CR 734 to Paradise Basin. Drive 2.3 miles to Paradise Pass. Turn right (W) at Yule Pass sign. There are three roads. Turn right, (NE) and drive 0.2 miles further to a parking area. Hike west up the old mining road. There is a trailhead sign ahead.

Trail Description

There is no trailhead sign for this hike. It heads north, up a steep dirt path, right from the parking area. Starting at 11,315 feet, it ascends almost 1,000 feet in less than a mile. This well defined trail disappears after 0.2 miles. Just as it ends, there is a small cairn **17** on the left (W) side of the trail. Go straight ahead at this cairn (N), gradually climbing from one bench to another. At some point, the hillside offers an opportunity to switchback to the southwest while still climbing at a moderate grade.

You reach a wide, obvious bench **18** at about 0.5 miles. Look west and up to the main, steep ridgeline that leads directly to the summit. Hikers have cut a trail straight up that ridge. It is extremely steep and strenuous. It is hard to get good footing. Coming down it is equally difficult. Look right (N). A long, easy ascending

Hiking the ridgeline

depression goes straight north, towards the lower end of the peak's north ridgeline. This is a much easier route to ascend and descend. Follow the depression. You should come upon a deep mine shaft **19** where the depression and the ridgeline meet. Turn left (W) and climb 0.1 miles to the high ridge. This is the steepest part, but the talus is soft, making footholds easier.

Once you have reached the long ridgeline **20**, it is an easy ascent to the summit **21**. The views are 360 degrees. The scenic rewards have accompanied you all the way, from the very start to the magical summit. What a hike!

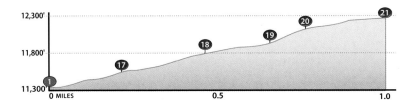

GPS	Mile	Latitude	Longitude	Elevation	Comment
1	0.0	38,59,28N	107,3,57W	11,315'	Start Paradise Pass to Cinnamon Mountain.
17	0.18	38,59,36N	107,3,54W	11,460'	Cairn. Trail disappears. Go north.
18	0.43	38,59,41N	107,4,1W	11,746'	Wide bench. Go right (N) up depression.
19	0.64	38,59,51N	107,4,2W	11,911'	Old mine shaft.
20	0.72	38,59,52N	107,4,7W	12,086'	North end of Cinnamon Ridge.
21	0.97	38,59,41N	107,4,15W	12,286'	Summit Cinnamon Mountain.

Black line is more moderate route than red.

20

19

18

17

Start of Hike

Washington Gulch

Washington Gulch is really a very short valley compared to the others. Its greatness stems from being completely surrounded by peaks. Though there are fewer trailheads (6 total) accessed from Washington Gulch, all but the Snodgrass hike start very high in elevation. Views are, therefore, instant. The trails are short, and vary from easy to difficult. Passenger cars can easily access 4 of the hikes (28-31).

Washington Gulch road also connects with Gothic Road and Slate River Road via Paradise Basin Road. These loops are best driven with high clearance vehicles. There are long stretches of the road that are only one lane–wide and hang high along steep cliffs. Backing up may be necessary.

Looking down Washington Gulch Valley

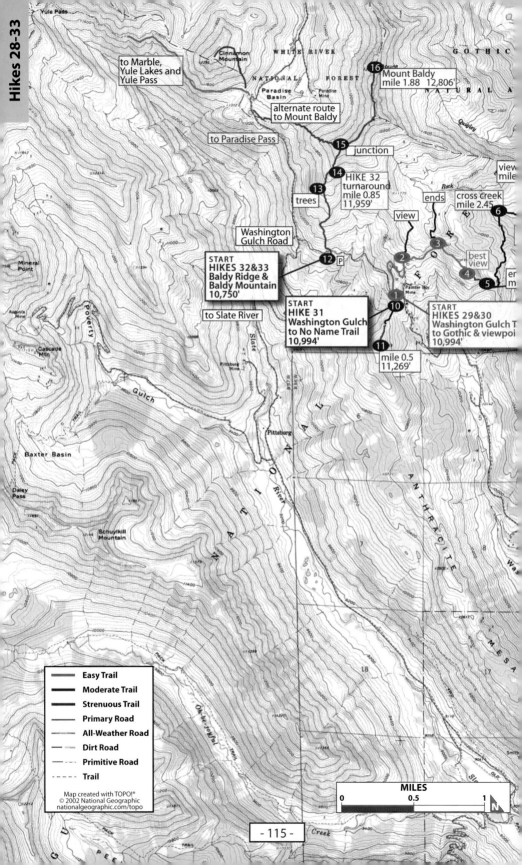

to Marble,
Yule Lakes and
Yule Pass

16 Mount Baldy
mile 1.88 12,806'

alternate route
to Mount Baldy

to Paradise Pass

15 junction

14 HIKE 32
turnaround
mile 0.85
11,959'

13 trees

ends

view

cross creek
mile 2.45

6

view
mile

2

3

best
view

4

5

er
m

Washington
Gulch Road

12 P

START
HIKES 32&33
Baldy Ridge &
Baldy Mountain
10,750'

to Slate River

START
HIKE 31
Washington Gulch
to No Name Trail
10,994'

1

10

START
HIKES 29&30
Washington Gulch T
to Gothic & viewpoi
10,994'

11

mile 0.5
11,269'

Mineral
Point

Poverty

Augusta
Mine

Cascade
Mtn

Pittsburg
Mine

Baxter Basin

Daisy
Pass

Pittsburg

Schuylkill
Mountain

WHITE RIVER

Cinnamon
Mountain

NATIONAL   FOREST

Paradise
Basin

Paradise
Mine

GOTHIC

NATURAL A

Quigley

Rock

Painter Boy
Mine

Slate River

Gulch

NATIONAL

ANTHRACITE

MESA

Legend	
——	Easy Trail
——	Moderate Trail
——	Strenuous Trail
——	Primary Road
——	All-Weather Road
– – –	Dirt Road
–·–·–	Primitive Road
- - -	Trail

Map created with TOPO!®
© 2002 National Geographic
nationalgeographic.com/topo

MILES

0   0.5   1

N

Creek

FOLLOW THE GPS POINTS

Hike 28 - Snodgrass, 17-22, SHUTTLE

Hike 29 - Washington Gulch to Viewpoint, 1-4, RETURN

Hike 30 - Washington Gulch to Gothic, 1-9, SHUTTLE

Hike 31 - No Name Hike, 10, 11, RETURN

Hike 32 - Baldy Ridge, 12-14, RETURN

Hike 33 - Mount Baldy, 12-16, RETURN

END
HIKE 30
mile 4.0
9,667'

to Crested Butte
Gothic Road CR 317

Gothic

Gothic
Mountain

junction
mile 2.91

START
HIKE 28
Snodgrass
9,506'

highest elevation
mile 2.28   9,967'

junction
mile 3.37

END
HIKE 28
mile 3.53
9,573'

start views of
Mt Crested Butte
mile 1.68   9,766'

to Crested Butte
Washington Gulch Road
CR 811

to Crested Butte
Gothic Road CR 317

28

Snodgrass Trail

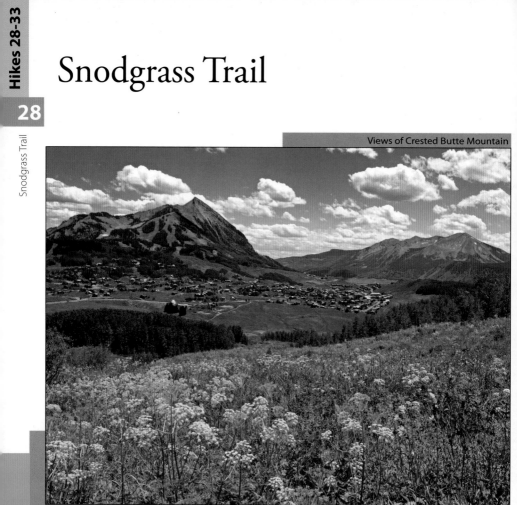

Views of Crested Butte Mountain

Distance	3.53 miles from start to shuttle point.
Difficulty Rating	Easy to moderate.
Surface	Easy packed dirt all the way.
Gradient	Easy to mile 1.68; moderate to finish.
Average Time	2 hours, 30 minutes.
Elevations	TH: 9,506; Highest: 9,967; Gain: +567
Maps	Latitude 40 Crested Butte, Taylor Park;
	Trails Illustrated 131 & 133. Trail 590
Star Rating	

Highlights

Cross easy benchland for 3 miles, taking in unparalleled views of Mount Bellview, Hike through beautiful aspen forest and wildflower meadows with views of numerous peaks. Wonderful, expansive vistas of Crested Butte and the entire valley below.

> **Directions To Trailhead:** From CBVC, drive 1.75 miles north on CR 317 to Washington Gulch Road CR 811. Turn left (W) and drive 3 miles to marked trailhead on right (N) side of road. There is a small parking area just past the trailhead.

> **Shuttle:** From CBVC, drive north 4.25 miles on CR 317. Just past the horse stables, there is a large parking area on the left (W) where the trail begins or ends.

Trail Description

Bikers and hikers alike share this very popular trail. Be aware that the trail has seasonal closures (in the fall). The trailhead sign will inform you of dates. You can hike in either direction, but we prefer to start in Washington Gulch because the uphill gradient is easier from this approach. The trail begins in open seasonally flower-filled meadows, then enters young aspen forest.

After hiking about 1.68 miles **18**, the trail opens to more continuous vistas overlooking Crested Butte and the valley below. This point also marks the beginning of steep but short ups and downs that turn the easy trail to moderate. In season, wildflowers smother the open hillsides all the way to the finish.

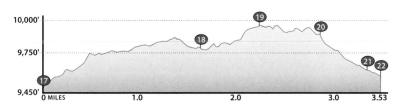

Trail starts in open meadow

Views along trail through aspen

Aspen forest

GPS	Mile	Latitude	Longitude	Elevation	Comment
17	0.0	38,55,22N	107,0,17W	9,506'	Start Snodgrass Trail.
18	1.68	38,54,51N	106,59,2W	9,766'	Start views of Crested Butte.
19	2.28	38,55,9N	106,58,41W	9,967'	Highest elevation point.
20	2.91	38,55,23N	106,58,10W	9,876'	Junction: cross over the style.
21	3.37	38,55,14N	106,57,47W	9,637'	Junction to horse corrals. Go straight.
22	3.53	38,55,10N	106,57,37W	9,573'	Finish Snodgrass Trail.

Washington Gulch to Viewpoint

Views from beginning of trail

Distance	2.66 miles out & back.
Difficulty Rating	Easy.
Surface	Easy packed dirt.
Gradient	Mostly easy.
Average Time	1 hour, 30 minutes.
Elevations	TH: 10,994; Highest: 11,423; Gain: +480
Maps	Latitude 40 Crested Butte, Taylor Park;
	Trails Illustrated 133. Trail 403
Star Rating	

Highlights

This is a high altitude hike with various vistas of peaks and valleys from start to finish on a short, easy trail. See northern peaks of the Ruby Range, Mount Baldy, Gothic Mountain, and down the valley to Crested Butte. Superb opportunities for dramatic photography.

> Directions To Trailhead: From CBVC, drive 1.75 miles north on CR 317 to Washington Gulch Road CR 811. Drive 7.76 miles to signed trailhead with ample parking. Cars can drive to this trailhead. Tight turn for vehicles over 20 feet upon approaching the summit.

Trail Description

The start of this hike is about 11,000 feet. Though the trail is easy, the altitude may add a new level of difficulty for some folks. Adjust this easy rating accordingly.

The parking area for this hike offers a view down the entire Washington Valley all the way to Crested Butte. It has great photographic potential, especially in the later afternoon, and may be worth another drive up when the light is accommodating.

From the trailhead, there are immediate views of the northern Ruby Range. The trail climbs easily to a vista overlooking Washington Valley, then climbs through a meadow of colorful seasonal flowers. At mile 0.7 **2**, there is an unmarked fork in the trail. The straight trail (N) goes uphill for 0.27 miles. It ends at a wonderful viewpoint of Mount Baldy and the Gothic Valley. It is a nice side trip.

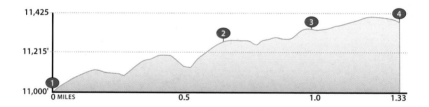

Otherwise, take the right fork (E) to continue on Washington Gulch Trail. Then wind into a gully and encounter a short, difficult side hill. At mile 1.06 **3**, you reach a vista point where you can see Gothic Valley. To your left is Mount Baldy; to the right is Gothic Mountain.

This is also a beautiful place to photograph, but you are not at the best viewpoint yet. Take the right fork (SE) 0.35 miles further to arrive at the panoramic scenic vista **4**. This is the turnaround point for hike 29.

Second viewpoint

GPS	Mile	Latitude	Longitude	Elevation	Comment
1	0.0	38,58,3N	107,2,34W	10,994'	Start Washington Gulchl to Viewpoint.
2	0.70	38,58,19N	107,2,31W	11,279'	Unmarked fork in trail. Go right(E).
3	1.06	38,58,25N	107,2,11W	11,339'	Go right (SE) for best viewpoint.
4	1.33	38,58,14N	107,1,53W	11,423'	Summit. Turnaround.

Destination viewpoint

Washington Gulch to
30 Gothic

One viewpoint near top of pass

Distance	4 miles one way to shuttle point.
Difficulty Rating	Moderate to difficult after leaving summit at mile 1.41
Surface	Mostly rocky with bike trenches after leaving summit.
Gradient	Mostly very steep after leaving summit, but downhill.
Elevations	TH: 10,994; Highest: 11,423; Gain: +549; Loss: -1,935
Maps	Latitude 40 Crested Butte, Taylor Park;
	Trails Illustrated 133. Trail 403
Star Rating	

Highlights

From the start to the viewpoint, peaks dominate the horizon. After the summit, the best vistas are from mile 3 to the end. The trail switchbacks down through waist-high flowers in season, and the Gothic Valley peaks crowd the horizon with greens, reds and grays.

Directions To Trailhead: From CBVC, drive 1.75 miles north on CR 317 to Washington Gulch Road CR 811. Drive 7.76 miles to signed trailhead with ample parking. Cars can drive to this trailhead. Tight turn for vehicles over 20 feet upon approaching the summit.

Shuttle: From CBVC, drive north 9.83 miles on Gothic Road CR 317 to the signed Washington Gulch trailhead, where there is parking. Cars can access this shuttle.

Trail Description

Read the description for hike 29 to the viewpoint **4**. After leaving this viewpoint, the trail descends a very steep, slippery slope. There are excellent views of Gothic Mountain from here.

At mile 1.6 **5**, enter dense spruce forest. There are no views until mile 2.45, where you cross Rock Creek **6** and enter a meadow. Wildflowers are not as prolific here compared to those you will see farther below, but the views of Gothic Mountain and Avery Peak are well framed by evergreens **7**. From here, the trail meanders in and out of spruce and meadow with partial views of different peaks. It is not as steep through this section.

Views of Gothic Mountain

View of Gothic Valley near trail's end

The end of the trail, **8** to **9** is the best scenically. In season, the wildflowers grow waist high and frame exceptional views up and down Gothic Valley. This is also the most difficult section of the trail. It is very steep and rocky, and bicycles have cut a narrow trench that makes finding stable footing a challenge.

Another option for this trail is to hike up one mile from Gothic Road to see the flowers and return the way you came. The trail is very steep from this side.

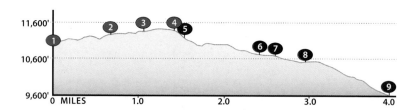

GPS	Mile	Latitude	Longitude	Elevation	Comment
1	0.0	38,58,3N	107,2,34W	10,994'	Start Washington Gulch to Gothic.
2	0.70	38,58,19N	107,2,31W	11,279'	Unmarked fork in trail. Go right (E)
3	1.06	38,58,25N	107,2,11W	11,339'	Unmarked fork in trail. Go right (E).
4	1.33	38,58,14N	107,1,53W	11,423'	Summit. Panoramic vistas.
5	1.60	38,58,9N	107,1,45W	11,128'	Enter spruce forest to GPS 7.
6	2.45	38,58,38N	107,1,36W	10,717'	Cross creek. Enter meadow.
7	2.63	38,58,35N	107,1,23W	10,709'	Views of Avery Peak and Gothic Mountain.
8	3.00	38,58,49N	107,1,7W	10,534'	Views of Gothic Valley to end of trail.
9	4.00	38,58,55N	107,0,26W	9,667'	End Washington Gulch to Gothic.

Washington Gulch
No Name Trail

Views from top

Distance	1 mile out & back.
Difficulty Rating	Sustained moderate.
Surface	Packed dirt and some rock.
Gradient	Sustained moderate to steep.
Average Time	45 minutes.
Elevations	TH: 10,994; Highest: 11,269; Gain: +320
Maps	Latitude 40 Crested Butte, Taylor Park.
	No trail marked on any map.
Star Rating	

Highlights

Short hike that packs a scenic punch. Views, views, and more views in all directions. Just about every peak and trail we describe can be located from this little knob. Amazing!

> Directions To Trailhead: From CBVC, drive 1.75 miles north on CR 317 to Washington Gulch Road CR 811. Drive 7.76 miles to signed trailhead with ample parking. Cars can drive to this trailhead. Tight turn for vehicles over 20 feet upon approaching the summit.

Trail Description

Short, and oh so sweet. No trail name. No trail sign. Walk out towards the campfires near the large parking area for Washington Gulch Trail 403. You can see the trail heading straight up to a little knob. It gets a little steep towards the second part. Remember the altitude. That's it!

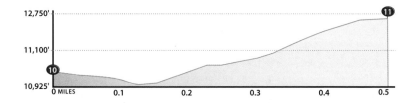

GPS	Mile	Latitude	Longitude	Elevation	Comment
10	0.0	38,58,3N	107,2,34W	10,994'	Start Washington Gulch No Name Trail.
11	0.50	38,57,41N	107,2,45W	11,269'	Enjoy!

Trail ascends knob

Baldy Ridge

View of Yule Pass from Baldy Ridge

Distance	1.7 miles out & back.
Difficulty Rating	Sustained moderate to difficult.
Surface	Alpine grass and flowers.
Gradient	Sustained moderate with steep start.
Average Time	2 hours.
Elevations	TH: 10,750; Highest: 11,959; Gain +1,200
Maps	Latitude 40 Crested Butte, Taylor Park. Off-trail.
Star Rating	

Highlights

This is a short off-trail hike with astounding views down Washington Valley to Crested Butte, Gothic Mountain, and the Slate River peaks. Afternoon light is best for photos.

> **Directions To Trailhead:**
> From CBVC, drive 1.75 miles north on CR 317 to Washington Gulch Road CR 811. Drive 8.51 miles north (0.75 miles beyond pass) to an unmarked single vehicle pulloff spot opposite where the ridgeline meets the road. SUV recommended after Washington Gulch Pass.

Trail Description

This is a marvelous opportunity for hikers who would like to try an off-trail experience without going a long distance. Employ route finding and map reading skills, while being able to see your destination. Use the photos we took for additional aid. If you have a GPS, load our waypoints and practice tracking. (A GPS will also aid in finding the starting point!) The shorter vegetation is easier to walk through than the tall flowers of Gothic Valley. The route starts up a steep bank, and then becomes a steady climb. The wide ridgeline meanders its way to the scrub trees **13** just below the steep, rocky ridge, which is your turnaround point. Choose your route depending upon how steeply you wish to ascend. Washington Valley and the peaks of Gothic Valley and Slate River Valley come into view as you climb. Once on the ridge, there are great views of Yule Pass as well.

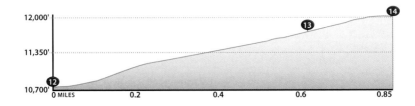

GPS	Mile	Latitude	Longitude	Elevation	Comment
12	0.0	38,58,20N	107,3,10W	10,750'	Start Baldy Ridge.
13	0.68	38,58,48N	107,3,14W	11,704'	Arrive at scrub trees on main ridgeline.
14	0.85	38,58,55N	107,3,9W	11,959'	Turnaround point where tundra turns to broken rock and the ridge is very steep.

Trail ascends knob

Turnaround at treeline

Mount Baldy

Distance	3.76 miles out & back.
Difficulty Rating	Difficult.
Surface	Alpine tundra and talus slopes.
Gradient	Sustained moderate to tree line. Very steep to ridge top. Moderate to pe
Average Time	5 hours.
Elevations	TH: 10,750; Highest: 12,806; Gain: +2,132
Maps	Latitude 40 Crested Butte, Taylor Park. Off trail.
Star Rating	

Snowmass Wilderness & Baldy Ridge

Highlights

Incredible views of Snowmass Mountain and the peaks of the Snowmass Wilderness Area, Yule Pass, Cinnamon Mountain, and the Washington and Slate River Valleys. This is special.

Directions To Trailhead: From CBVC, drive 1.75 miles north on CR 317 to Washington Gulch Road CR 811. Drive 8.51 miles north (0.75 miles beyond pass) to an unmarked single vehicle pulloff spot opposite where the ridgeline meets the road. SUV recommended after Washington Gulch Pass.

View towards Yule Pass & Cinnamon Mountain

Trail Description

Read the description for hike 32 to ⑭. Once above tree line, the route becomes very steep, climbing on loose talus and larger rock fall. It is very strenuous. There is an occasional, faint trail up this portion. Finally, you reach a high point where the vistas now include looking out over Paradise Pass and Yule Pass.

At ⑮, take note that another ridge line, with a better trail than what you came up, leads steeply down to Paradise Pass. This is a steeper, though shorter, approach to Mount Baldy. Be aware when returning not to follow this more evident trail. We did! That's how we know where it goes! It separates you from your vehicle by another 2.5 miles! There is still more climbing to do, but once above this junction the gradient mellows out enough to become sustained moderate, and there is a well defined trail. Still, we show the route as difficult. It is very rocky, and extremely narrow. We encountered strong winds that were very threatening because the drop was straight down. A storm was moving in, so we retreated after about halfway out.

On a good weather day, however, the magnificent peaks of the Snowmass Wilderness Area will stand above all others. Being on this narrow ridge is like clinging to the head of a pin with your toenails. The rest of the world starts below your feet.

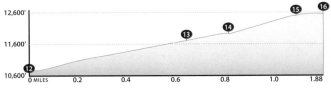

Route up ridge from Washington Gulch side

GPS	Mile	Latitude	Longitude	Elevation	Comment
12	0.0	38,58,20N	107,3,10W	10,750'	Parking spot on Washington Gulch Road. Start Mount Baldy.
13	0.68	38,58,48N	107,3,14W	11,704'	Arrive at scrub trees on ridge line.
14	0.85	38,58,55N	107,3,9W	11,959'	Start steep ascent on talus slopes.
15	1.10	38,59,6N	107,3,4W	12,471"	Unmarked junction: to Paradise Pass.
16	1.88	38,59,37N	107,2,46W	12,806'	Mount Baldy summit.

View of Washington Gulch Valley

Slate River Valley

On first impression, the Slate River Valley seems quite tame. The 2-wheel drive dirt road meanders from Crested Butte through small housing developments and grazing land that soon spreads into wide, flower strewn meadows. As the mountainous walls begin closing in, questions arise. Where could hiking trails possibly go from here? The answer of course is up, up into the Ruby Range that separates Slate River Valley from Kebler Pass. These 4 hikes are long and require stamina. Three hikes go to high passes. The trails saunter, if you will, through long valleys, before hitting the steep walls that border them. Then the trails climb. It is a drier valley. The wildflowers are not as prolific, though still very pretty in season. A high clearance vehicle is recommended to access all these trailheads.

You can climb the steep walls

in your car as well. The valley hits a wall at its northwest end, and the road is forced to switchback up to the top of the Anthracite Mesa, where you have a choice of taking the Washington Gulch Road back home or continuing up to Paradise Divide and crossing over to Schofield Pass.

Slate River Valley

START
HIKE 37
Daisy Pass Trail to
Oh Be Joyful TH
9,777'

17

Leave road,
go left on trail
10,783'

16

Baxter Basin

15 Daisy Pass
11,644'

Augusta
Mountain

Mineral
Point

Augusta
Mine

Angel
Pass

Richmond
Mtn

Demo̶rat Basin

Schuylkill
Mountain

Oh Be Joyful Pass
mile 6.34 11,779'

14

Oh-be-joyful
Pass

13

no junction
10,885'

Swan
Basin

Hancock
Peak

Dippold
Basin

Oh Be
Joyful
Creek
10,070'

6

Hike 34 turnaround
Oh Be Joyful Creek
mile 3.33 9,980'

5

Buck
Basin

Buck
Basin

'Oh-be-joyful
Peak

Little
Silver Basin

junction
10,514'

7

Silver
Basin

Afley
Peak

Silver
Basin

Blue Lake

8

9

Blue Lake
mile 5.5
11,078'

Garfield
Summit
mile 6.68
12,079'

12 Garfield
Peak

10

11

Star Pass
mile 6.47
11,872'

Peele̶
Peak

Mount
Owen

Green Lake

Robinson
Basin

GUNNISON

SCARP

PEELE

Ruby
Peak

Spring

	Easy Trail
	Moderate Trail
	Strenuous Trail
	Primary Road
	All-Weather Road
	Dirt Road
	Primitive Road
	Trail

Map created with TOPO!®
© 2002 National Geographic
nationalgeographic.com/topo

FOLLOW THE GPS POINTS

Hike 34 - Oh Be Joyful to Meadows View, 1-5, RETURN

Hike 35 - Oh Be Joyful to Blue Lake & Garfield, 1-12, RETURN

Hike 36 - Oh Be Joyful Pass, 1-7, 13, 14, RETURN

Hike 37 - Daisy Pass to Oh Be Joyful TH, 17-15, 13, 7-1, SHUTTLE

Poverty
Gulch Rd
4WD
2.05 miles
to TH

Gothic
Mountain

Slate River Road
CR 734

unmarked junction
to Oh Be Joyful TH

4WD only
0.8 miles to TH

junction
to Gunsight
Pass

TH sign

wilderness
9,559'

END
HIKE 37
mile 8.62

START
HIKES 34-36
9,295'

to Crested Butte

MILES

0   0.5   1

34

Oh Be Joyful to Meadows View

Distance	6.66 miles out & back.
Difficulty Rating	Easy.
Surface	Mostly easy packed dirt.
Gradient	Easy.
Average Time	4 hours.
Elevations	TH: 9,295; Highest: 9,980; Gain: +662
Maps	Latitude 40 Crested Butte, Taylor Park;
	Trails Illustrated 133. Trail 406
Star Rating	

Highlights

An easy trail ascending a wide, sunny valley surrounded by dramatic peaks. In season, wildflowers bloom across these meadows.

Directions To Trailhead: From CBVC, drive north 0.83 miles on CR 317 to Slate River Road. Turn left (NW) and drive the dirt road 4.6 miles to the unmarked junction to Slate River Campsite. Drive down the rough road to the camp, cross the Slate River (check depth), and drive the very narrow, high clearance road another 0.8 miles to a flat grassy area to park. You'll need 4X4 beyond this point. (If you park at the river, add 1.6 miles and 350 feet of elevation to the hike.)

Trail Description

From the upper parking spot, walk the remaining 0.33 miles to the actual trailhead sign **2**. The trail starts out rocky and rough, improving at 0.9 miles **3**. By mile 1.45 **4**, you have entered the sunny, spacious meadows typical of this valley and can see some of the peaks at the far end. In prime flower season, these meadows are bright yellow. As you proceed up valley, the peaks become more prominent. It is a long, leisurely hike all the way to the first crossing of Oh Be Joyful Creek at mile 3.33 **5**, which is a good turnaround point.

Entering open meadows typical of this valley

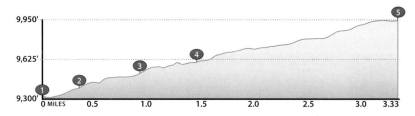

GPS	Mile	Latitude	Longitude	Elevation	Comment
1	0.0	38,54,30N	107,2,35W	9,295'	Start Oh Be Joyful to Meadows View from upper parking spot.
2	0.33	38,54,28N	107,2,55W	9,373'	Trailhead sign. Distances are incorrect.
3	0.90	38,54,29N	107,3,29W	9,559'	Wilderness sign.
4	1.45	38,54,46N	107,3,57W	9,593'	Enter meadows. Views of peaks.
5	3.33	38,55,43N	107,5,22W	9,980'	Oh Be Joyful Creek. Turnaround point.

Oh Be Joyful to Blue Lake & Garfield Peak

Distance	Out & Back. Blue Lake: 11 miles; Garfield Peak: 13.36 miles.
Difficulty Rating	Moderate with one short, steep climb to Star Pass.
Surface	Mostly easy packed dirt to mile 3.78. Mostly broken rock to lake.
Gradient	Easy to mile 3.78. Moderate to lake. Steep 0.14 miles to Star Pass.
Average Time	6 hours, 30 minutes to Blue Lake; 9 hours to Garfield Peak.
Elevations	TH: 9,295; Highest: 11,078 or 12,079; Gain: +1,780 or + 2,701
Maps	Latitude 40 Crested Butte, Taylor Park; Trails Illustrated 133. Trails 406 to 404
Star Rating	

Highlights

Blue Lake, a pristine alpine lake, nestles directly below the cliff face of Scarp Ridge with wide open views across Oh Be Joyful Valley. Spectacular vistas from the summit of Garfield Peak looking back to Scarp Ridge and its surrounding peaks, down Peeler Valley to Gunsight Pass, and across the Slate River and Gothic Valleys to the Maroon Bells Wilderness. Once at Blue Lake, this is an easy peak ascent.

Blue Lake

Directions To Trailhead: From CBVC, drive north 0.83 miles on CR 317 to Slate River Road. Turn left (NW) and drive the dirt road 4.6 miles to the unmarked junction to Slate River Campsite. Drive down the rough road to the camp, cross the Slate River (check depth), and drive the very narrow, high clearance road another 0.8 miles to a flat grassy area to park. You'll need 4X4 beyond this point. (If you park at the river, add 1.6 miles and 350 feet of elevation to the hike.)

Trail Description

The first 1.45 miles is through spruce forest, then the trail suddenly enters meadowland with views of the distant peaks **4**. It is an easy jaunt across these meadows to mile 3.78 **6**, when you cross Oh Be Joyful Creek for the second time. The trail turns to moderate and enters the trees again. At mile 4.36 **7**, there is a junction sign that indicates Daisy Pass and Gunsight Pass. Go left (S) to Gunsight Pass to go to Blue Lake. The lake is a gem nestled against the sheer cliffs of Scarp Ridge **9**.

View of Blue Lake from Star Pass

If you decide to continue to Star Pass and Garfield Peak, it is a relatively easy ascent except for the extremely steep 0.14 miles to gain the saddle at Star Pass. There is no trail to follow from the lake. The destination is obvious; the saddle at Star Pass is dead ahead, and you will intersect the steep trail heading to that pass **10**. The loose talus is annoying, as backward slippage easily occurs. At the saddle **11**, the trail continues for a while into Peeler Basin, but soon fades. Instead of following it, turn left (N) and start the ascent to Garfield Peak summit. The actual walk up the wide, rocky slope from the saddle is very easy. From the top **12**, the views are equal to the two Scarp Ridge hikes.

GPS	Mile	Latitude	Longitude	Elevation	Comment
1	0.0	38,54,30N	107,2,35W	9,295'	Start Oh Be Joyful to Blue Lake & Garfield Peak.
2	0.33	38,54,28N	107,2,55W	9,373'	Trailhead sign. Distances are incorrect.
3	0.90	38,54,29N	107,3,29W	9,559'	Wilderness sign.
4	1.45	38,54,46N	107,3,57W	9,593'	Enter meadows. Views of peaks.
5	3.33	38,55,43N	107,5,22W	9,980'	Cross Oh Be Joyful Creek.
6	3.78	38,55,38N	107,5,50W	10,070'	Cross OBJ Creek again. Trail turns moderate.
7	4.36	38,55,33N	107,6,20W	10,514'	Junction: go left (S) for Blue Lake.
8	5.14	38,55,0N	107,6,25W	10,798'	Junction: stay on main trail to lake.
9	5.5	38,54,55N	107,6,41W	11,078'	Blue Lake.
10	6.33	38,54,50N	107,5,54W	11,588'	Junction: Star Pass Trail. Start steep climb.
11	6.47	38,54,44N	107,5,50W	11,872'	Star Pass. Turn left (N) for peak ascent.
12	6.68	38,54,54N	107,5,46W	12,079'	Summit Garfield Peak.

View from Garfield Peak

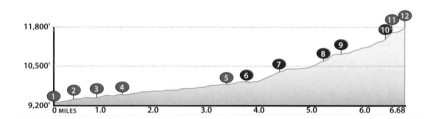

View of Peeler Basin from Star Pass

Oh Be Joyful to Oh Be Joyful Pass

36

View towards Kebler Pass area from summit

Distance	12.68 miles out & back.
Difficulty Rating	Moderate with 3.78 miles of easy.
Surface	Mostly easy packed dirt to mile 3.78. Mostly broken rock to summit.
Gradient	Easy to mile 3.78. Moderate to summit.
Average Time	8 hours, 30 minutes.
Elevations	TH; 9,295; Highest: 11,779; Gain: +2,430
Maps	Latitude 40 Crested Butte, Taylor Park; Trails Illustrated 133. Trail 406.
Star Rating	

Highlights

The Oh Be Joyful valley is completely surrounded by dramatic peaks and ridges. Democrat Basin is a classic high altitude glacial basin. Expansive views from Oh be Joyful Pass over the Kebler Pass side and across to Daisy Pass.

> **Directions To Trailhead:** From CBVC, drive north 0.83 miles on CR 317 to Slate River Road. Turn left (NW) and drive the dirt road 4.6 miles to the unmarked junction to Slate River Campsite. Drive down the rough road to the camp, cross the Slate River (check depth), and drive the very narrow, high clearance road another 0.8 miles to a flat grassy area to park. You'll need 4X4 beyond this point. (If you park at the river, add 1.6 miles and 350 feet of elevation to the hike.)

Trail Description

Read the description for hike 35 to **7**, then continue with the following.

Go straight (N), following the sign to Daisy Pass. The trail climbs 0.3 miles, topping out at a dramatic viewpoint of Democrat Basin.

The trail meanders through the basin. All the trail maps show another junction at about mile 5.34 **13**, north going to Daisy Pass, and west to Oh Be Joyful Pass. We found a cairn at about the correct spot, but no hint of any trail going to Daisy Pass. The only visible part of that trail is where it switchbacks up the mountain to Daisy Pass itself.

After this non-existent junction, the trail climbs seriously for the final mile to Oh Be Joyful Pass **14**. It gains 894 feet and is the toughest part of the trail, but the views down and across valley, and the vistas gained from the summit, far exceed the effort.

View from summit across Daisy Pass

Entering Democrat Basin

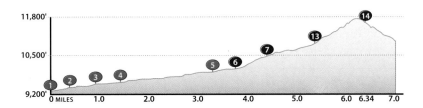

GPS	Mile	Latitude	Longitude	Elevation	Comment
1	0.0	38,54,30N	107,2,35W	9,295'	Start Oh Be Joyful to Oh Be Joyful Pass
2	0.33	38,54,28N	107,2,55W	9,373'	Trailhead sign. Distances are incorrect.
3	0.90	38,54,29N	107,3,29W	9,559'	Wilderness sign.
4	1.45	38,54,46N	107,3,57W	9,593'	Enter meadows. Views of peaks.
5	3.33	38,55,43N	107,5,22W	9,980'	Cross Oh Be Joyful Creek.
6	3.78	38,55,38N	107,5,50W	10,070'	Cross Oh Be Joyful Creek again.
7	4.36	38,55,33N	107,6,20W	10,514'	Junction: Oh Be Joyful & Blue Lake.
13	5.34	38,56,19N	107,6,27W	10,885'	Junction on map not there.
14	6.34	38,56,22N	107,6,55W	11,779'	Summit Oh Be Joyful Pass.

Daisy Pass to Oh Be Joyful Trailhead

View from Daisy Pass to Gothic Valley

Distance	8.62 miles one way to shuttle. River crossing shoes recommended.
Difficulty Rating	Moderate, with 0.76 miles of difficult and 3.45 miles of easy.
Surface	Mostly loose talus, some alpine tundra. Easy packed dirt last 3.45 miles.
Gradient	Moderate, with 0.76 very steep and 3.45 miles of very easy.
Average Time	7 hours.
Elevations	TH: 9,777; Highest: 11,644; Gain: +1,849; Loss: -2,291
Maps	Latitude 40 Crested Butte, Taylor Park; Trails Illustrated 133. Trails 404 to 406
Star Rating	

Highlights

From Daisy Pass summit, views extend north to the Maroon Bells, east to the peaks lining Gothic Valley, and southwest into the Oh Be Joyful valley ringed by the Ragged Wilderness peaks. The trail continues through Democrat Basin's lakes and tundra, then descends along Oh Be Joyful Creek as it cuts through meadows of seasonal wildflowers.

Directions To Trailhead: From CBVC, drive north 0.83 miles on CR 317 to Slate River Road. Turn left (NW) and drive the dirt road 7.17 miles to Poverty Gulch Road. Turn left (W) and cross the Slate River (check depth). The road is narrow and rocky; high clearance vehicle recommended. Drive 2.05 miles to where the road crosses the creek. Park on the near side. Do not drive across the creek.

Shuttle: From CBVC, drive north 0.83 miles on CR 317 to Slate River Road. Turn left (NW) and drive the dirt road 4.6 miles to the unmarked junction to Slate River Campsite. Drive down the rough road to the camp, cross the Slate River (check depth), and drive the very narrow, high clearance road another 0.8 miles to a flat grassy area to park. We recommend 4X4 beyond this point.

Author near start of hike

Descending Daisy Pass

Trail Description

Cross Poverty Creek (crossing shoes may be necessary), and head up the old, unmaintained mining road to Baxter Basin. The trail is very rocky, but not too steep. There are few wildflowers in this basin, and even fewer trees of any variety. It is the dryer side of the mountain, and though the flanks are covered with greenery it has a barren, rocky feeling in comparison to the fertile Gothic Valley.

A foot trail (user sign, but no trail name) leaves the road at mile 1.64 **16**. This trail is narrow, very rocky and gets steeper as you ascend. There are two gully crossings high up that are washed away, and finding good footing is difficult. The loose rock on steep sections may be strenuous.

The summit of Daisy Pass **15** is about 15 feet wide. The other side descends precipitously into Democrat Basin.

As you descend, it would be a good idea to survey your route. Once at the bottom of the switchbacks, your trail will disappear. From your lofty perch, search out the best route across Democrat Basin to the other side. In order to intersect the Oh Be Joyful Trail, you want to pass below the steep rock cliffs that border two ponds. Do

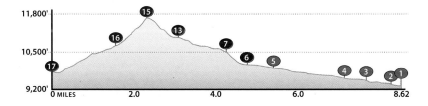

not turn down valley until you have hiked to the far side. Otherwise, you may get caught on the north side of Oh Be Joyful Creek. As it descends, the banks get very steep and difficult to cross.

Once you have connected with Oh Be Joyful trail, it travels down Democrat Basin and descends a short, steeper section to the signed junction **7** to Gunsight Pass. Turn left (E) and begin a moderate descent through spruce forest to Oh Be Joyful Creek. It is an easy hike through meadows from the creek to the finish.

Constantly look behind as you travel down. The views of this ring of mountain peaks will stay with you until the very last mile of the entire journey.

Hikers descend the Oh Be Joyful Valley

View up valley near the end of the trail

GPS	Mile	Latitude	Longitude	Elevation	Comment
17	0.0	38,57,38N	107,5,17W	9,777'	Start Daisy Pass to OBJ
16	1.64	38,57,6N	107,6,0W	10,783'	Take foot trail left (south).
15	2.40	38,56,44N	107,6,9W	11,644'	Daisy Pass summit.
13	3.18	38,56,19N	107,6,27W	10,885'	Junction on map only.
7	4.28	38,55,33N	107,6,20W	10,514'	Junction: to Blue Lake.
6	4.86	38,55,38N	107,5,50W	10,070'	Cross Oh Be Joyful Creek.
5	5.31	38,55,43N	107,5,22W	9,980'	Cross Oh Be Joyful Creek.
4	7.17	38,54,46N	107,3,57W	9,593'	Enter spruce. Last views.
3	7.67	38,54,29N	107,3,29W	9,559'	Leaving Ragged Wilderness.
2	8.25	38,54,28N	107,2,55W	9,373'	Distances on TH sign are incorrect.
1	8.62	38,54,30N	107,2,35W	9,295'	Park shuttle vehicle here.

Kebler Pass

Kebler Pass is the place to hike for exhilarating fall aspen color. A good quality dirt road, for cars as well as trailers, leads right out of Crested Butte and crosses over 10,007-foot high Kebler Pass to CO 133 and Paonia. Most of its 32-mile length offers showstopper scenery. Winding above and through the largest contiguous aspen forest in the US, it draws photographers, nature lovers and surprised tourists into its embrace. As you drive from east to west, the Ragged Wilderness borders the north side of Kebler Pass, and the West Elk Wilderness the south side. The mountains are single, massive monoliths, as well as mountain chains, rising dramatically above the meadows and forests.

An abundance of stunning, primitive free campsites permit longer visits for the wilderness hungry crowd. Eighteen hikes are accessible from this road.

View from Kebler Pass Road

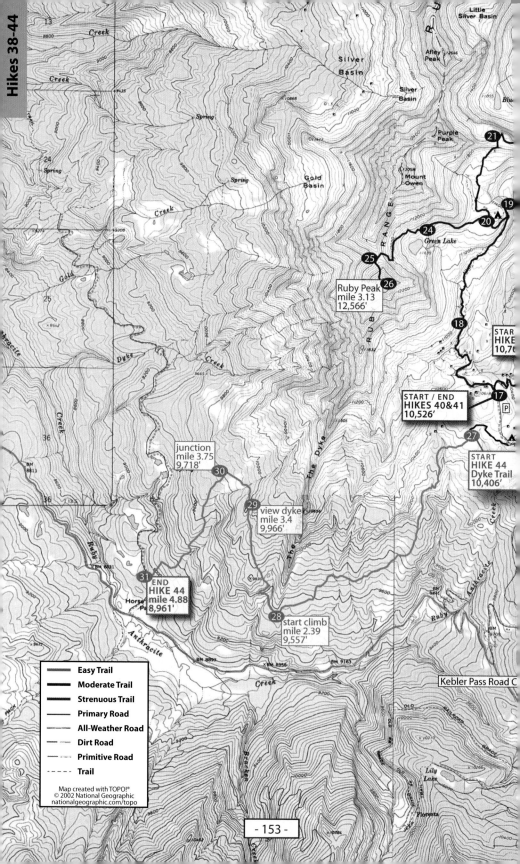

Silver Basin

Little Silver Basin

Afley Peak

Silver Basin

Purple Peak

21

Mount Owen

19

20

RANGE

24

Green Lake

25

26

Ruby Peak
mile 3.13
12,566'

RUB

18

START
HIKE
10,7

17

START / END
HIKES 40&41
10,526'

P

27

START
HIKE 44
Dyke Trail
10,406'

junction
mile 3.75
9,718'

30

29

view dyke
mile 3.4
9,966'

The Dyke

31

END
HIKE 44
mile 4.88
8,961'

Horse Pa

28

start climb
mile 2.39
9,557'

Anthracite

Kebler Pass Road C

Lily Lake

Floresta

Legend:

Easy Trail	
Moderate Trail	
Strenuous Trail	
Primary Road	
All-Weather Road	
Dirt Road	
Primitive Road	
Trail	

Map created with TOPO!®
© 2002 National Geographic
nationalgeographic.com/topo

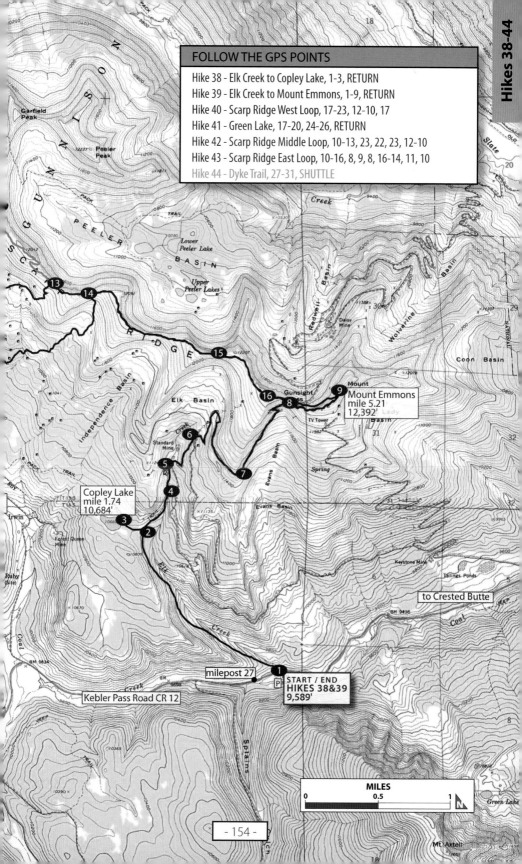

FOLLOW THE GPS POINTS

Hike 38 - Elk Creek to Copley Lake, 1-3, RETURN
Hike 39 - Elk Creek to Mount Emmons, 1-9, RETURN
Hike 40 - Scarp Ridge West Loop, 17-23, 12-10, 17
Hike 41 - Green Lake, 17-20, 24-26, RETURN
Hike 42 - Scarp Ridge Middle Loop, 10-13, 23, 22, 23, 12-10
Hike 43 - Scarp Ridge East Loop, 10-16, 8, 9, 8, 16-14, 11, 10
Hike 44 - Dyke Trail, 27-31, SHUTTLE

Mount Emmons
mile 5.21
12,392'

Copley Lake
mile 1.74
10,684'

to Crested Butte

milepost 27

START / END
HIKES 38&39
9,589'

Kebler Pass Road CR 12

MILES
0   0.5   1

Elk Creek to
Copley Lake

38

Copley Lake

Distance	3.48 miles out & back.
Difficulty Rating	Sustained moderate.
Surface	Mostly loose rock.
Gradient	Sustained moderate with steeper sections.
Average Time	2 hours, 30 minutes.
Elevations	TH: 9,589; Highest: 10,689; Gain: +1,115
Maps	Latitude 40 Crested Butte, Taylor Park;
	Latitude 40 Crested Butte, Taylor Park. Rd 826.1D
Star Rating	

GPS	Mile	Latitude	Longitude	Elevation	Comment
1	0.0	38,51,25N	107,3,36W	9,589'	Start Elk Creek to Copley Lake.
2	1.54	38,52,17N	107,4,43W	10,783'	Junction: to Copley Lake. Go north.
3	1.74	38,52,21N	107,4,54W	10,684'	Copley Lake.

Highlights

Copley Lake is surrounded by in-season wildflower meadows guarded by Ruby Peak and Mount Owen.

Directions To Trailhead: From CBVC, drive south on CO 135 to Whiterock Avenue. Turn right (W). Drive about 4.5 miles (past mile marker 28 on Kebler Pass Road). There is a small, unmarked parking area on the left. Walk west up the road about 20 feet. There are two unmarked trails. Take the left hand trail west of Elk Creek.

Trail Description

The trail begins with a slippery, steep, loose rock climb, then quickly becomes sustained moderate all the way to Copley Lake. The 1,115 foot elevation gain is considerable for the short distance of 1.74 miles, so moderate borders on steep for stretches. The trail is an old mining road through dense spruce forest with some openings.

Suddenly, the spruce trees give way to a small meadow. A minor foot path goes straight ahead (N) while the old road turns right (E). Follow the foot path north **2**, then west just 0.2 miles to Copley Lake.

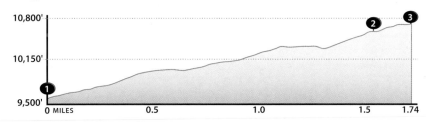

Much of the trail is through dense spruce

Some open areas along the trail

Elk Creek to
Mount Emmons

39

Distance	10.42 miles out & back to Mount Emmons.
Difficulty Rating	Sustained moderate with difficult section.
Surface	Mostly loose rock. Packed gravel along short sections of mining road.
Gradient	Sustained moderate with steep sections.
Average Time	6 hours, 30 minutes.
Elevations	TH: 9,589; Highest; 12,392; Gain: +2,970
Maps	Latitude 40 Crested Butte, Taylor Park. Rd 826.1D & trail 585
Star Rating	

View from Mount Emmons

Highlights

From Gunsight Pass to the summit of Mount Emmons, the 360 degree vistas of classic Colorado peaks spread out as far as the eye can see. This is the easiest peak to ascend, once you get to Gunsight Pass.

Directions To Trailhead: From CBVC, drive south on CO 135 to Whiterock Avenue. Turn right (W). Drive about 4.5 miles (past mile marker 28 on Kebler Pass Road). There is a small, unmarked parking area on the left. Walk west up the road about 20 feet. There are two unmarked trails. Take the left hand trail west of Elk Creek.

Trail Description

Read the description for hike 38 to **2**, then follow below.

From the junction with Copley Lake, follow the old road east and cross Elk Creek at mile 2.25 **4**. Ascend a steep hill. You will see an old trailer under a shed roof on your left. About 50 feet past this trailer, the trail meets a very good gravel road. This is one of several junctions you will want to make note of for the return trip.

Walk past Standard Mine property

It is easy to miss the little trail on the way back **5**. Take the good gravel road to the left. Immediately, you will come upon the unmarked entrance to the former Standard Mine.

Stay on the main road as it turns right, then switchbacks left, passing above Standard Mine's little building. Soon, there is another junction **6** . This time, the main road goes right, while you want to take the smaller road that goes up the hill, next to the gully devastated by mining activity, and begins a series of long switchbacks. Follow this road into Elk Basin, where you now have a sweeping view looking up at Scarp Ridge.

This is not wilderness area, however. The effects of years of mining are all around. Follow the switchback, so evident on the map. The road turns to single

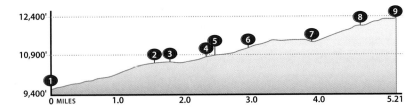

View from Gunsight Pass of Oh Be Joyful

track and you have your first real good views into the Kebler Pass area.

At mile 3.88 **7**, you have your first view of Gunsight Pass and Mount Emmons. The long ascent to the pass is across ankle twisting rock, and is the steepest section of the trail.

From Gunsight Pass **8**, the views into the Slate River Valley are spectacular. The jeep road you see plummeting down the north side of Gunsight Pass is 5 miles of broken rock that makes walking very difficult and unpleasant. It ends at Slate River Campground.

If you look west at the steep cliff rising above Gunsight Pass, you will spot a faint trail that climbs the cliff to Scarp Ridge. This connects to Scarp Ridge East Loop **16**, which is a 6 star route to Gunsight Pass and Mount Emmons.

At Gunsight Pass, walk around the locked gate to ascend Mount Emmons. The trail is very obvious and quite easy. It is the easiest peak to ascend and is the best part of this hike. From the summit **9**, you can see every valley and peak described in this book.

Views towards Kebler Pass area

Climb to Gunsight Pass

GPS	Mile	Latitude	Longitude	Elevation	Comment
1	0.0	38,51,25N	107,3,36W	9,589'	Start Elk Creek to Mount Emmons
2	1.54	38,52,17N	107,4,43W	10,783'	Junction: to Copley Lake.
3	1.74	38,52,21N	107,4,54W	10,684'	Copley Lake.
4	2.25	38,52,32N	107,4,31W	10,768'	Cross Elk Creek.
5	2.45	38,52,42N	107,4,29W	10,934'	Junction: go left on this gravel road.
6	2.97	38,52,53N	107,4,17W	11,222'	Junction: go straight uphill. Do not go right.
7	3.88	38,52,39N	107,3,55W	11,509'	View of Gunsight Pass & Mount Emmons.
8	4.67	38,53,6N	107,3,30W	12,090'	Gunsight Pass.
9	5.21	38,53,12N	107,3,4W	12,392'	Summit Mount Emmons.

Scarp Ridge West Loop

Distance	6.73–mile loop.
Difficulty Rating	Moderate with strenuous sections.
Surface	Mostly small loose rock on packed dirt.
Gradient	Mostly moderate with three very steep sections.
Average Time	4 hours, 30 minutes.
Elevations	TH: 10,526; Highest: 12,202; Gain: +1,897
Maps	Latitude 40 Crested Butte, Taylor Park. RD 826.1D & Trail 419
Star Rating	☆☆☆☆☆☆☆

Ascending view looking back

Highlights

Views, views, and more views in every direction of classic Colorado scenery, including the peaks and meadows of the West Elk Wilderness, the Ragged Wilderness, the Maroon Bells-Snowmass Wilderness, and the Collegiate Wilderness. The entire hike from start to finish is a photographer's list of superlatives. The hike follows the ridgeline for approximately one mile before starting the equally scenic descent to Lake Irwin Lodge.

Directions To Trailhead: From CBVC, drive 6.95 miles on Kebler Pass Road CR 12 to turnoff for Lake Irwin Campground. Drive 2.56 miles. Drive past campground entrance. Road is rocky; cars may scrape. At mile 2.91, turn right (N) at the fork. Park at mile 3.19, by the unmarked log entrance to Lake Irwin Lodge. SUVs can proceed up the road 2.11 more miles and do a shorter out & back hike as an option.

Trail Description

The trail begins on a 4x4 road **17** . After the road crosses a stream **18** , the views really expand. A waterfall thunders down from Green Lake high above. Up, up, up, at a moderate gradient, each step elevating the drama of the views until the road's end **20** .

You have reached an alpine basin at the base of Mount Owen and Ruby and Purple Peaks. An unmarked trail forks left (W) to Green Lake and Ruby Peak (hike 41). Go right, following the faint trail northwesterly as it winds its way through the wildflowers and streams of this luxuriant alpine landscape. Scarp Ridge is always in your view.

From the ridge **21**, sheer cliffs drop off 2,000 feet to the north. Immediately below is Oh-Be-Joyful Basin. Democrat Basin, ringed by the peaks of the Ragged Wilderness, is farther up the valley. The Maroon Bells dominate the northern view.

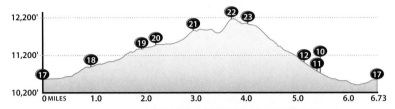

The backbone of Scarp ridge

Views of Blue Lake from Scarp Ridge

To the east is the backbone of Scarp Ridge heading towards Gunsight Pass.

The trail along the spine of Scarp Ridge has many steep and narrow sections. Loose talus makes parts slippery as well. Just when you think you have reached the top, you have to descend about 80 feet before making the final ascent of 400 feet to the real summit **22**. From the summit, the trail descends moderately at first, then steeply as it turns toward the Lake Irwin Lodge far below **10**. Expansive views accompany you all the way. Once at the lodge, a road takes you down and up a ravine and finally back to your vehicle.

Viewpoint along ascending road

Steep part of ridge

GPS	Mile	Latitude	Longitude	Elevation	Comment
17	0.0	38,53,8,N	107,6,41,W	10,526'	Start Scarp Ridge West Loop.
18	0.95	38,53,35,N	107,6,58W	10,871'	Road crosses creek. Views expand.
19	1.95	38,54,19N	107,6,38W	11,375'	Special viewpoint.
20	2.11	38,54,14,N	107,6,46,W	11,476'	End 4x4 road. Junction: to Green Lake. Go North.
21	2.97	38,54,45,N	107,6,41,W	11,866'	Arrive at Scarp Ridge.
22	3.76	38,54,34,N	107,6,0,W	12,202'	Highest point on Scarp Ridge.
23	4.12	38,54,19N	107,5,57W	12,031'	Unmarked trail to East Loop.
12	5.26	38,53,26N	107,6,1W	11,010'	Unmarked trail to East Loop.
11	5.51	38,53,15N	107,6,3W	10,742'	Junction: return from East Loop.
10	5.59	38,53,13,N	107,6,8,W	10,695'	Lake Irwin Lodge.
17	6.73	38,53,8,N	107,6,41,W	10,526'	Finish Scarp Ridge West Loop.

Green Lake and Ruby Peak

Distance	6.26 miles out & back.
Difficulty Rating	Sustained moderate.
Surface	Mostly small loose rock on packed dirt.
Gradient	Sustained moderate.
Average Time	3 hours, 30 minutes.
Elevations	TH: 10,526; Highest: 12,566; Gain: +2,040
Maps	Latitude 40 Crested Butte, Taylor Park.
	RD 826.1D. No numbers to peak.
Star Rating	☆☆☆☆☆☆☆

Highlights

An unbelievable old mining road climbs to the saddle between Ruby Peak and Mount Owen, offering spectacular views of Green Lake below, with Scarp Ridge in the distance, along with East Beckwith and Marcellina Mountains in the Kebler Valley. The ascent to Ruby Peak is moderate, and worth the added effort.

Directions To Trailhead: From CBVC, drive 6.95 miles on Kebler Pass Road CR 12 to turnoff for Lake Irwin Campground. Drive 2.56 miles. Drive past campground entrance. Road is rocky; cars may scrape. At mile 2.91, turn right (N) at the fork. Park at mile 3.19, by the unmarked log entrance to Lake Irwin Lodge. SUVs can proceed up the road 2.11 more miles and do a shorter out & back hike as an option.

Trail Description

Read the description for hike 40 to **20** , then follow below.

The trail to Green Lake and Ruby Peak is easily visible from the alpine basin. It is etched into the red rock of Ruby Peak, traversing the steep slopes as it heads for the obvious saddle. Take the left (W) fork **20** . The right fork goes to Scarp Ridge.

You can see where Green Lake should be. Soon, it comes into view **24** . The name is a bit of a misnomer; the lake is as blue as a lake could possibly be. Continuing

Waterfall along route

up, you should see a shortcut trail that saves hiking the long, last switchback. Walk directly up to the saddle. From the saddle **25** , the views of East Beckwith and Marcellina Mountains up Kebler Valley add to what you have been seeing behind. In fall, the aspens on this latter side wrap the peaks in yellow aprons. It is easy to see the trail leading up to Ruby Peak **26** . Considering time and energy spent getting here, it is an easy peak to ascend.

Remember the waterfall you saw tumbling out of Green Lake as you were hiking up the trail? A very pleasant, off trail shortcut along the big, flat bench below Green Lake is an alternative way to return. After passing the lake **24** , pick your way across the flat bench. Follow the stream until it plummets over the ledge. There are different routes down, around the various falls, and many photographic opportunities. The old road that takes you back to the starting point is always in view along this shortcut.

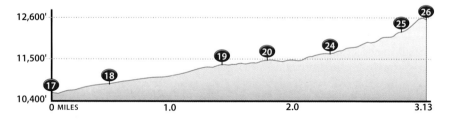

Green Lake with Lake Irwin below

GPS	Mile	Latitude	Longitude	Elevation	Comment
17	0.0	38,53,15N	107,7,1W	10,594'	Start Green Lake & Ruby Peak
18	0.48	38,53,35N	107,6,58W	10,871'	Road crosses creek. Vistas expand.
19	1.5	38,54,19N	107,6,38W	11,375'	Special viewpoint.
20	1.8	38,54,10N	107,6,46W	11,476'	End 4x4 road. Junction: to Green Lake.
24	2.32	38,54,10N	107,7,18W	11,689'	Green Lake.
25	2.9	38,54,59N	107,7,42W	12,218'	Saddle between Ruby Peak & Mount Owen.
26	3.13	38,53,50N	107,7,38W	12,566'	Ruby Peak.

Alpine Basin. Road leads to pass.

Scarp Ridge Middle Loop

Distance	4.31–mile loop.

Difficulty Rating	Sustained moderate if loop is hiked counterclockwise.
Surface	Mostly small loose rock on packed dirt.
Gradient	Mostly sustained moderate.
Average Time	3 hours.
Elevations	TH 10,695; Highest: 12,202; Gain: +1,523
Maps	Latitude 40 Crested Butte, Taylor Park. Trail 421 to trail 419
Star Rating	

View from Scarp Ridge

Highlights

This hike goes to the same summit view as the Scarp Ridge West hike, but is shorter and avoids the steepest and most narrow parts of the ridge. It follows the ridgeline further east and opens up spectacular views into Peeler Basin.

Directions To Trailhead: From CBVC, drive 6.95 miles west on Kebler Pass Road CR 12 to the turnoff for Lake Irwin Campground. Drive 2.56 miles. Drive past the campground entrance. The road is rocky; cars may scrape. At top of hill (2.91 miles), turn right (N) at the fork. Drive uphill to the unmarked log entrance gate to Lake Irwin Lodge. Drive 1 mile to the lodge. There is a trailhead sign nailed to a tree on the west side of the lodge.

Trail Description

This route is sustained moderate if you follow the loop counterclockwise. The ascent is much steeper going clockwise. After the first 200 yards, the trail ascends straight up the hill with no switchbacks. Be aware of when you reach the first level part of this ascent. An unmarked, well disguised trail **12** takes off across a rock slab, just before the trail crosses a flat wash. You have not seen any slab rock before this point. Walk across the slab. On the far side (just 50 feet further), the trail is visible. You should be heading up a valley in an easterly direction. If you miss this junction, you will be heading westerly.

The trail climbs through meadows, up a small ravine. Excellent views of Lake Irwin appear behind you. As you climb, you can see Scarp Ridge above. At mile 1.37 **13** , another unmarked trail heads east. This goes to Gunsight Pass. For now, go left (NW). In another 0.3 miles, you will reach the ridge top, where the views overlooking the mountain ranges stretch to the far horizon.

Hike up the ridge. The trail fades in and out, as few hikers know this route. The views are riveting. In about 0.85 miles, you will cross the main trail from the lodge **23** . That is your return route. The summit of Scarp Ridge is 0.3 miles further west. Be sure to continue to this summit **22** before returning, as the views there are excellent.

To complete the loop, backtrack down the trail to **23** . Stay on the main trail. This trail descends moderately at first, then steeply as it turns toward the Lake Irwin Lodge far below. Expansive views accompany you all the way to your vehicle.

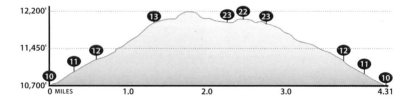

Descending the loop

GPS	Mile	Latitude	Longitude	Elevation	Comment
10	0.00	38,53,13N	107,6,8W	10,695'	Start hike at lodge.
11	0.30	38,53,15N	107,6,3W	10,742'	Junction: return trail from East Loop.
12	0.80	38,53,26N	107,6,1W	11,010'	Barley visible junction. Cross rock slab.
13	1.37	38,53,50N	107,5,29W	11,885'	Junction: to Gunsight Pass. Go left (NW).
23	2.22	38,54,19N	107,5,57W	12,031'	Merge with main trail. Go straight (N).
22	2.50	38,54,34N	107,6,0,W	12,202'	Summit Scarp Ridge.
23	2.81	38,54,19N	107,5,57W	12,031'	Take main trail downhill.
12	3.50	38,53,26N	107.6.1W	11,010'	Merge with Middle Loop. Go downhill.
11	3.97	38,53,15N	107,6,3W	10,742'	Junction: return trail from East Loop.
10	4.31	38,53,13N	107,6,8W	10,695'	Finish hike at lodge.

Hiking the ridge

Scarp Ridge East to Mount Emmons

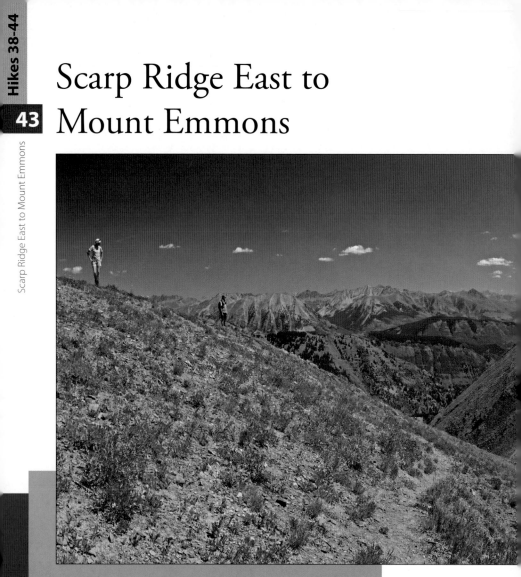

Distance	7.9 miles out & back . Go out Scarp Ridge any distance you prefer.
Difficulty Rating	Sustained moderate.
Surface	Alternating small loose rock and packed dirt.
Gradient	Sustained moderate with some steeper sections.
Average Time	5 hours.
Elevations	: TH: 10,695; Highest; 12,392; Gain: +2,726
Maps	Latitude 40 Crested Butte, Taylor Park. Trail 421; no trail on map to Gunsight.
Star Rating	

View from Scarp Ridge

Highlights

Like the Scarp Ridge West and Middle hikes, the 360 degree vistas from this magnificent ridge are classic Colorado. This trail follows the ridge for the longest distance of the Scarp Ridge choices. It is not shown on any maps.

Directions To Trailhead: From CBVC, drive 6.95 miles west on Kebler Pass Road CR 12 to the turnoff for Lake Irwin Campground. Drive 2.56 miles. Drive past the campground entrance. The road is rocky; cars may scrape. At top of hill (2.91 miles), turn right (N) at the fork. Drive uphill to the unmarked log entrance gate to Lake Irwin Lodge. Drive 1 mile to the lodge. There is a trailhead sign nailed to a tree on the west side of the lodge.

Trail Description

Follow the description for hike 42 to **13**, then continue below.

At **13**, you intersect another unmarked trail heading east up a steep slope through dense, low brush. Take this trail. Once you have hiked through the brush,

you will be standing on the precipice of Scarp Ridge overlooking the upper end of Peeler Basin. Wow!

The trail dips and climbs all the way to Mount Emmons. Views are in every direction, as the ridge is very narrow in various sections. Sometimes the trail is faint, but it is easy to see where you are headed. The steepest part is after reaching the ridge summit **16**. The trail descends to Gunsight Pass **8**, then climbs easily to summit Mount Emmons **9**. We prefer this hike to reach Emmons over hike 39, which follows old roads through spruce forest.

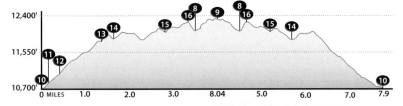

Descending to Gunsight Pass

On returning, you may wish to hike the eastern leg of the loop where **14** shows on the map. It saves going up the last big hill to **13** and is the same mileage. There is no junction here, and the trail is faint at first, but just go down the steep slope. The lower portion of this trail passes through more spruce forest than going back the way you came.

Views on both sides of ridge

GPS	Mile	Latitude	Longitude	Elevation	Comment
10	0.0	38,53,13N	107,6,8W	10,695'	Start Scarp Ridge East.
11	0.3	38,53,15N	107,6,3W	10,742'	Junction: go left. The dirt path is the return trail.
12	0.8	38,53,26N	107,6,1W	11,010'	Barley visible junction. Cross rock slab.
13	1.35	38,53,50N	107,5,29W	11,885'	Junction: to Gunsight Pass. Go right (E).
14	1.67	38,53,46N	107,5,9W	11,889'	Junction: this is the return trail.
15	2.84	38,53,24N	107,4,6W	12,079'	Narrow ridge. View into Elk Creek Basin.
16	3.42	38,53,8N	107,3,39W	12,314'	Summit Scarp Ridge.
8	3.57	38,53,6N	107,3,30W	12,090'	Gunsight Pass.
9	3.95	38,53,12N	107,3,4W	12,392'	Mount Emmons.
8	4.54	38,53,6N	107,3,30W	12,090'	Gunsight Pass.
16	4.72	38,53,8N	107,3,39W	12,314'	Summit Scarp Ridge.
15	5.28	38,53,24N	107,4,6W	12,079'	Narrow ridge. View into Elk Creek Basin.
14	6.46	38,53,46N	107,5,9W	11,889'	Junction: this is the return trail.
10	7.90	38,53,13N	107,6,8W	10,695'	Finish hike at lodge.

Ascending East Loop trail. Views of Ruby Peak

Dyke Trail

View of the Dyke and Ruby Peak

Distance	4.88 miles from start to shuttle point.
Difficulty Rating	Easy.
Surface	Easy packed dirt most of the way.
Gradient	Easy downhill except for a short ascent of 598 feet.
Average Time	2 hours.
Elevations	TH: 10,407; Highest: 10,407; Gain: +598; Loss: -2,029
Maps	Latitude 40 Aspen, Crested Butte, Gunnison;
	Trails Illustrated 133. Trails 837 to 833
Star Rating	

GPS	Mile	Latitude	Longitude	Elevation	Comment
27	0.0	38,52,52N	107,6,55W	10,407'	Start Dyke Trail.
28	2.39	38,51,45N	107,8,30W	9,557'	Begin only climb in trail.
29	3.4	38,52,26N	107,8,45W	9,966'	View of The Dyke.
30	3.75	38,52,38N	107,8,56W	9,718'	Junction to Lake Irwin Trail.
31	4.88	38,51,59N	107,9,33W	8,961'	Finish Dyke Trail.

Highlights

Fall color makes this hike a beautiful walk through pristine aspen forest. Excellent views of Kebler Pass area at the beginning of the hike.

Directions To Trailhead: From CBVC, drive 6.95 miles west on Kebler Pass Road CR 12 to the turnoff for Lake Irwin. Drive 2.56 miles. Go past campground. Road is rocky; cars may scrape. At mile 2.91 is a fork in road. Drive the smaller, left fork (W) 1 mile to signed trailhead.

Shuttle: From CBVC, drive Kebler Pass Road CR 12 west to milepost 20. Turn right (NE) into Horse Ranch Park. Drive past outhouse 0.1 miles to trailhead sign. Ample parking.

Trail Description

The Dyke hike is one of the most popular bicycling trails in the area. Weekends are especially busy with bicycle traffic. Hikers might wish to be aware of this.

The trail is almost entirely through very pretty aspen forest. There are a few openings with views of the surrounding mountains. At mile 3.4 **29** , there are very good views of The Dyke and East Beckwith Mountain. The trail is mostly easy packed dirt, and mostly downhill which makes for a very pleasant forest walk.

Walk is primarily through aspen forest

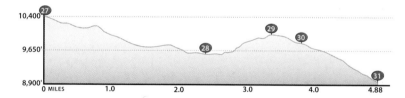

View from start of hike

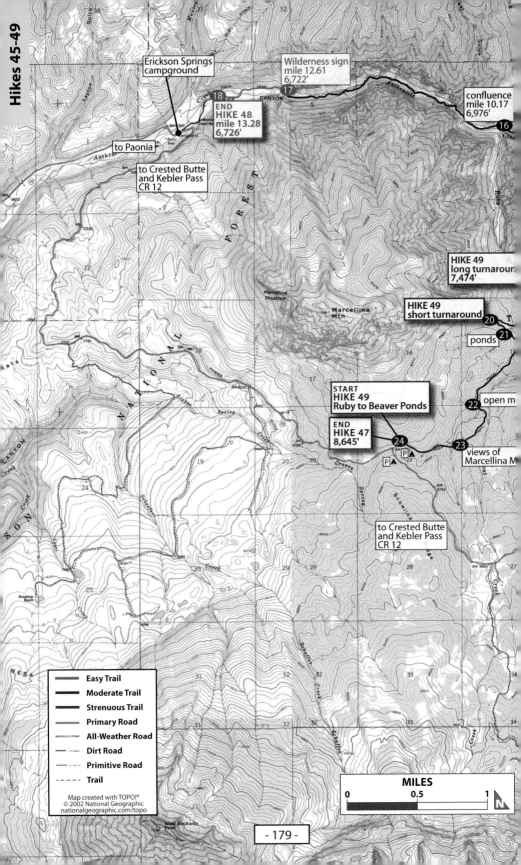

Erickson Springs campground

Wilderness sign
mile 12.61
6,722'

confluence
mile 10.17
6,976'

18

17

16

END
HIKE 48
mile 13.28
6,726'

to Paonia

to Crested Butte
and Kebler Pass
CR 12

FOREST

HIKE 49
long turnaround
7,474'

HIKE 49
short turnaround

20

21

ponds

Marcellina
Mountain

Marcellina
Mtn

START
HIKE 49
Ruby to Beaver Ponds

open m

END
HIKE 47
8,645'

22

24

23

views of
Marcellina M

NATIONAL

to Crested Butte
and Kebler Pass
CR 12

MESA

Easy Trail
Moderate Trail
Strenuous Trail
Primary Road
All-Weather Road
Dirt Road
Primitive Road
Trail

MILES

0   0.5   1

N

Map created with TOPO!®
© 2002 National Geographic
nationalgeographic.com/topo

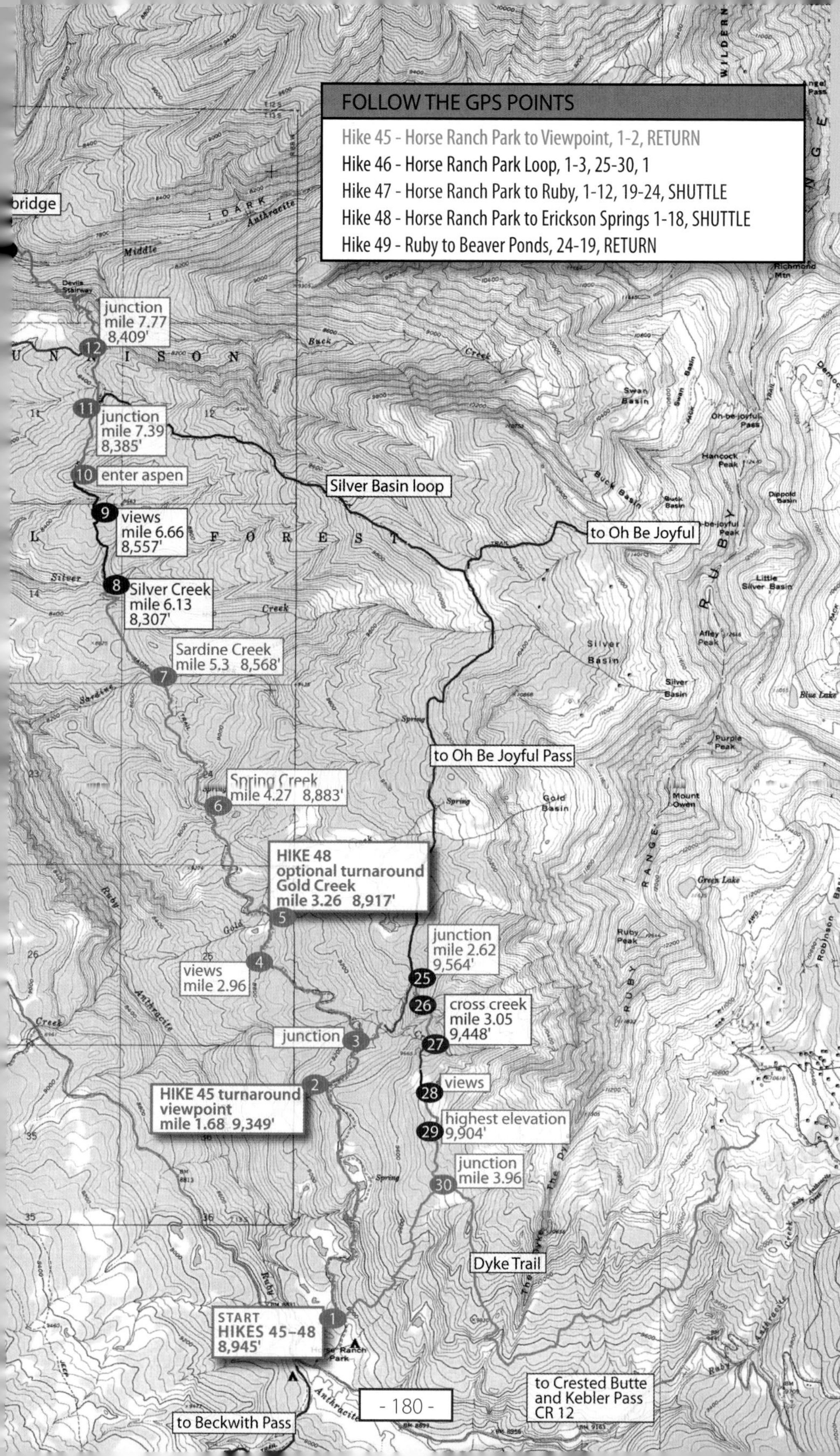

FOLLOW THE GPS POINTS
Hike 45 - Horse Ranch Park to Viewpoint, 1-2, RETURN
Hike 46 - Horse Ranch Park Loop, 1-3, 25-30, 1
Hike 47 - Horse Ranch Park to Ruby, 1-12, 19-24, SHUTTLE
Hike 48 - Horse Ranch Park to Erickson Springs 1-18, SHUTTLE
Hike 49 - Ruby to Beaver Ponds, 24-19, RETURN
bridge
junction mile 7.77 8,409'
junction mile 7.39 8,385'
enter aspen
Silver Basin loop
views mile 6.66 8,557'
to Oh Be Joyful
Silver Creek mile 6.13 8,307'
Sardine Creek mile 5.3 8,568'
to Oh Be Joyful Pass
Spring Creek mile 4.27 8,883'
HIKE 48 optional turnaround Gold Creek mile 3.26 8,917'
junction mile 2.62 9,564'
views mile 2.96
cross creek mile 3.05 9,448'
junction
HIKE 45 turnaround viewpoint mile 1.68 9,349'
views
highest elevation 9,904'
junction mile 3.96
Dyke Trail
START HIKES 45–48 8,945'
to Crested Butte and Kebler Pass CR 12
to Beckwith Pass
Swan Basin
Oh-be-joyful Pass
Hancock Peak
Buck Basin
Silver Basin
Afley Peak
Little Silver Basin
Blue Lake
Purple Peak
Gold Basin
Mount Owen
Green Lake
Ruby Peak
Richmond Mtn
Democrat Basin
Horse Ranch Park
RUBY RANGE

Horse Ranch Park to Viewpoint

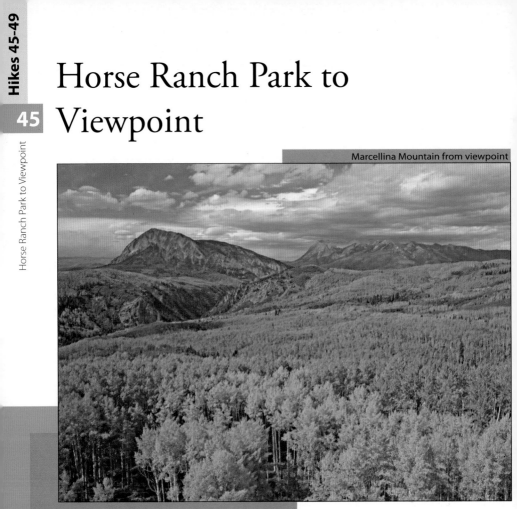

Marcellina Mountain from viewpoint

Distance	3.36 miles out & back.
Difficulty Rating	Easy.
Surface	Alternating easy packed dirt and loose rock.
Gradient	Mostly easy ascent.
Average Time	2 hours, 30 minutes.
Elevations	TH: 8,945; Highest: 9,349; Gain: +474
Maps	Latitude 40 Crested Butte, Taylor Park; Trails Illustrated 133. Trail 830
Star Rating	

GPS	Mile	Latitude	Longitude	Elevation	Comment
1	0.0	38,51,59N	107,9,34W	8,945'	Start Horse Ranch Park to Viewpoint.
2	1.68	38,53,6N	107,9,40W	9,349'	Best viewpoint. Turnaround point.

Highlights

This is the best short easy hike through beautiful aspen forest with multiple views along the way. The viewpoint at the turnaround encompasses Marcellina Mountain, the Ruby Range, both Beckwith peaks and so much more. Not to be missed. A photographer's delight.

Directions To Trailhead: From CBVC, drive 12.3 miles west on Kebler Pass Road CR 12. Turn right (N) into Horse Ranch Park. Drive past the outhouse 0.1 mile up the hill to trailhead parking. Cars can drive to this trailhead.

Trail Description

This is one of our favorite short hikes in the fall. There are many interesting viewpoints along the trail as it passes through very beautiful aspen forest. Each view offers a different perspective of the Kebler Pass mountains.

The trail climbs easily. Pass a large beaver lodge that seems to grow in size every year. Enter a series of large meadows with views of Ruby Peak and The Dyke, in addition to the views of East Beckwith Mountain that have accompanied you so far. Much of the aspen forest is mature; the tree trunks are thick and reflect a white to green color.

The most spectacular view, of course, is at the turnaround point. The trail leads out to a rock outcropping that allows a 180 degree view over the largest contiguous aspen forest in the country. There are too many peaks rising above this forest to name. Walk up the trail 100 yards further to a conspicuous rock pile. Climb around it and see even more of the Ruby Range.

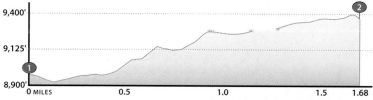

Vistas of East Beckwith Mountain along trail

Horse Ranch Park Loop

Meadow opens to views of Ruby Peak.

Distance	5.08-mile loop.
Difficulty Rating	Moderate with 2 steep, short climbs.
Surface	A mixture of rocky trail and packed dirt.
Gradient	Mostly moderate with some very steep, short sections.
Average Time	4 hours.
Elevations	TH: 8,945; Highest: 9,904; Gain: 1,424
Maps	Latitude 40 Crested Butte, Taylor Park;
	Trails Illustrated 133. Trails 830 to 834 to 837 to 838
Star Rating	☆☆☆☆☆

Highlights

This is a hike through beautiful aspen forest with many spectacular and varied views of Marcellina Mountain, Dark Canyon, and the Ragged Wilderness. Part of the largest contiguous aspen forest in the country. Wonderful display of fall colors.

> **Directions To Trailhead:** From CBVC, drive 12.3 miles west on Kebler Pass Road CR 12. Turn right (N) into Horse Ranch Park. Drive past the outhouse 0.1 mile up the hill to trailhead parking. Cars can drive to this trailhead.

Trail Description

Read the description for hike 45 to **2**.

From the viewpoint, continue down the trail to a junction **3**. Follow the sign to Oh Be Joyful Pass (NE). The trail ascends sharply, and footing is difficult. Then the climb eases until another junction **25**, where you take the right fork (E), following the sign to Lake Irwin Trail. Soon the trail cuts through a rock spine **26** and you are staring up at Ruby Peak bathed in golden aspen.

Descend steeply into a drainage **27**. There are incredible views of East Beckwith Mountain to your right, and Ruby Peak and the rock wall behind you. Then climb steeply out. Soon the trail breaks out into summer wildflower meadows. Leave the trail and wander about for special photo opportunities. This is where the photo, view midway along loop, was taken **28**.

Leaving this meadow, the trail tops out **29**, then descends easily to a massive talus slope that seems to have come from nowhere. Walk out to its edge for more

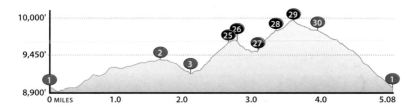

View midway along loop

magnificent views of East Beckwith Mountain, Marcellina Mountain, and beyond. Once you leave this spot, it is a short distance to the junction with the Dyke Trail **30** . Turn right (SE) into the aspen forest and descend 1.13 miles on an excellent packed dirt trail to your car.

Meadow opens to views of Ruby Peak

Views of Ruby Peak from talus slope

GPS	Mile	Latitude	Longitude	Elevation	Comment
1	0.0	38,51,59N	107,9,34W	8,945'	Start Horse Ranch Park Loop.
2	1.68	38,53,6N	107,9,40W	9,349'	Viewpoint.
3	2.11	38,53,18N	107,9,25W	9,160'	Junction: follow sign to Oh Be Joyful (E).
25	2.62	38,53,36N	107,9,7W	9,564'	Junction: follow sign to Lake Irwin (S).
26	2.79	38,53,28N	107,9,5W	9,555'	Cross rock spine.
27	3.05	38,53,18N	107,9,2W	9,448'	Cross creek. Begin climbing.
28	3.35	38,53,4N	107,9,3W	9,777'	Big meadows. Expansive views.
29	3.61	38,52,53N	107,8,59W	9,904'	Highest elevation.
30	3.96	38,52,38N	107,8,56W	9,718'	Junction: Dyke Trail. Go right.
1	5.08	38,51,59N	107,9,34W	8,945'	Finish Horse Ranch Park Loop.

Horse Ranch Park to Ruby Anthracite

Marcellina Mountain

Distance	12.32 miles from start to shuttle point. River crossing shoes recommended.
Difficulty Rating	Difficult.
Surface	Mostly easy packed dirt with some rocky and some slippery sections.
Gradient	Lots of easy downhill. Very steep descent and ascent to Ruby Anthracite Creek.
Average Time	9 hours.
Elevations	TH: 8,945; Highest; 9,349; Gain: +2,564; Loss: -2,923
Maps	Trails Illustrated 133. Trails 830 to 836
Star Rating	

Highlights

Aspens provide fall color. Frequent expansive 180 degree views of the Ruby Range, Marcellina Mountain, and the Anthracite Range throughout the entire hike. This is a feast for the senses. A must hike, especially in the fall.

> **Directions To Trailhead:** From CBVC, drive 12.3 miles west on Kebler Pass Road CR 12. Turn right (N) into Horse Ranch Park. Drive past the outhouse 0.1 mile up the hill to trailhead parking. Cars can drive to this trailhead.

> **Shuttle:** Drive west on Kebler Pass Road approximately 19.2 miles to milepost 14. Just beyond is a Forest Service sign for Ruby Anthracite Trail 836. Park across the road or take SUV up the road to the right (NE) another 0.1 miles to trailhead.

Trail Description

This hike is more difficult than hike 48 because of the steep climb out from Ruby Anthracite Creek. Read the description for hike 45 to **2** . From the viewpoint, hike 0.43 miles downhill to a junction **3** . Take the left fork to Erickson Springs.

The next 4 miles of easy descent has frequent, heart stopping big views. For hikers who wish to experience this wonderful trail but don't want to go through, consider turning around at mile 3.26 **5** , where the trail crosses Gold Creek. Beavers have built their pond across the trail. From there, you won't have too much climbing to get back.

After Gold Creek, the trail descends and ascends out of each subsequent drainage. There is a magnificent view of Marcellina Mountain just after Spring Creek **6** . Just past Sardine Creek **7** , another oak-covered hilltop offers more great photos. It is a longer descent, but still very gentle, down to Silver Creek **8** . You will know it by the log bridge built for hikers. The climb out of Silver Creek is narrow, rocky,

Beautiful aspen forest

East & West Beckwith Mountains

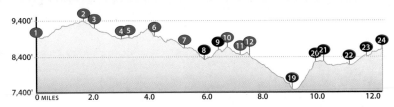

Beaver ponds

Drop into Anthracite Canyon

and steep. You may lose the trail in the sagebrush. Keep going towards the top of the hill. You will find the trail again. On this flat area **9** , there are 360 degree views of peaks wearing aprons of aspens. Above this bench, the trail crests, then drops into a beautiful aspen forest. The trees are tall and straight, their bark a soft green-white. It's magical. Descend through this forest to the junction for Silver Basin **11**. From here, it's a short jaunt to the next junction **12**. Turn left (S) on the Ruby Anthracite Trail.

This section is used infrequently. Descend the steep, slippery, overgrown trail into the canyon. Several lesser trails confuse the issue, but you can see your destination below. From the river, ascend 782 feet in 0.87 miles. When you reach the beaver ponds **20** , your major climbing is done.

These ponds deserve extra exploration. Mountain and fall aspen color reflecting in the water makes for special photos. After the beaver ponds, the trail climbs moderately through aspen forest for approximately 3 miles to your shuttle point. Views of the Ruby Range and Marcellina Mountain are behind you and to the right. High quality scenery all the way!

GPS	Mile	Latitude	Longitude	Elevation	Comment
1	0.0	38,51,59N	107,9,34W	8,945'	Start Horse Ranch Park to Ruby Anthracite.
2	1.68	38,53,6N	107,9,40W	9,349'	Fantastic views.
3	2.11	38,53,18N	107,9,25W	9,160'	Junction: Go left to Erickson Springs.
4	2.96	38,53,42N	107,10,2W	8,852'	Meadows with views.
5	3.26	38,53,54N	107,10,0W	8,917'	Gold Creek. Optional turnaround.
6	4.27	38,54,26N	107,10,25W	8,883'	Spring Creek. Great views just beyond.
7	5.3	38,55,3N	107,10,46W	8,568'	Sardine Creek. Good photos next hilltop.
8	6.13	38,55,29N	107,11,4W	8,307'	Silver Creek. Log bridge.
9	6.66	38,55,51N	107,11,9W	8,557'	360 degree views from hilltop.
10	6.96	38,56,2N	107,11,17W	8,614'	End difficult surface. Enter aspen.
11	7.39	38,56,21N	107,11,9W	8,385'	Junction: straight ahead to Erickson Springs.
12	7.77	38,56,39N	107,11,9W	8,409'	Junction: Left to Ruby Anthracite.
19	9.21	38,56,1N	107,12,27W	7,474'	Cross Ruby Anthracite Creek.
20	10.08	38,55,43N	107,12,50W	8,256'	Start beaver ponds.
21	10.26	38,55,37N	107,12,42W	8,194'	Leave beaver ponds.
22	11.16	38,55,2N	107,13,2W	8,179'	Meadows with views.
23	11.71	38,54,43N	107,13,17W	8,415'	Views of Marcellina Mountain.
24	12.32	38,54,44N	107,13,52W	8,645'	Finish.

Horse Ranch Park to Erickson Springs

Marcellina Mountain

Distance	13.28 miles from start to shuttle point.
Difficulty Rating	Moderate to difficult (due to rocky trail in canyon, and distance).
Surface	Mostly easy packed dirt to mile 6.13. Very rocky and muddy through canyon.
Gradient	Lots of easy downhill. Two moderate uphill sections.
Average Time	9 hours.
Elevations	TH: 8,945; Highest; 9,349; Gain: + 1,644; Loss: -3,793
Maps	Trails Illustrated 133. Trail 830
Star Rating	☆☆☆☆

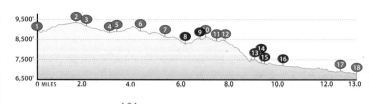

Highlights

This is a hike through beautiful aspen forest with many spectacular and varied vistas. Hike through two very different environments. Frequent expansive views of the Ruby Range, Marcellina Mountain, and the Anthracite Range while on the mesa. Dark Canyon is narrow, twisting, and intimate, with steep rock walls and thick vegetation enclosing the river. Especially picturesque in the fall.

> **Directions To Trailhead:** From CBVC, drive 12.3 miles west on Kebler Pass Road CR 12. Turn right (N) into Horse Ranch Park. Drive past the outhouse 0.1 mile up the hill to trailhead parking. Cars can drive to this trailhead.

> **Shuttle:** Drive west on Kebler Pass Road approximately 26.37 miles to Erickson Springs Campground. Drive northeast 0.5 miles to parking area at far end of campground.

Trail Description

This hike is easier than hike 47 because you don't have to climb out of the canyon after descending into it. Read the description for hike 47 to **12**. From the junction, descend 1,000 feet in 1.25 miles. This is the Devil's Staircase. Mathematically, this should be characterized as steep, but it is exceptionally easy. It is not a staircase at all. The grade is consistent, and the trail

Aspen forest

Confluence

is mostly packed dirt. The descent takes about 30 minutes.

The canyon walls are steep, bare rock, but the river valley is densely forested with aspens, gambrel oak, and other common brush varieties that turn color in fall. Views upward and outward are limited by the vegetation, as well as the steep canyon walls. The river flows clear, tumbling over rocks and gravel. This is a totally different hiking experience from

View of Beckwith Mountains

the dry, view-laden hillsides that you traversed to get here.

The trail hangs for a while about 50 feet above the creek. It is very rocky. Then the trail drops down to river level, where thick brush catches poles and deep mud hampers progress. Even though the gradient is gentle downhill, we slowed to an average of 1 mile per hour because of the trail conditions. When you reach the Wilderness sign **17** , the trail becomes broad and easy packed dirt to the finish.

Ruby Range appears frequently

Thick vegetation typical of the canyon section

GPS	Mile	Latitude	Longitude	Elevation	Comment
1	0.0	38,51,59N	107,9,34W	8,945'	Start Horse Ranch Park to Erickson Springs.
2	1.68	38,53,6N	107,9,40W	9,349'	Fantastic views.
3	2.11	38,53,18N	107,9,25W	9,160'	Junction: go left to Erickson Springs.
4	2.96	38,53,42N	107,10,2W	8,852'	Meadows with views.
5	3.26	38,53,54N	107,10,0W	8,917'	Gold Creek. Optional turnaround
6	4.27	38,54,26N	107,10,25W	8,883'	Spring Creek. Great views just beyond.
7	5.30	38,55,3N	107,10,46W	8,568'	Sardine Creek. Good photos next hilltop.
8	6.13	38,55,29N	107,11,4W	8,307'	Silver Creek. Log bridge.
9	6.66	38,55,51N	107,11,9W	8,557'	Panoramic views from hilltop.
10	6.96	38,56,2N	107,11,17W	8,614'	End difficult surface. Enter aspen.
11	7.39	38,56,21N	107,11,9W	8,385'	Junction: Straight ahead to Erickson Springs.
12	7.77	38,56,39N	107,11,9W	8,409'	Junction: Right to Erickson Springs.
13	9.03	38,57,7N	107,11,41W	7,530'	Bridge across Anthracite Creek.
14	9.34	38,57,16N	107,11,51W	7,308'	Bridge across North Anthracite Creek.
15	9.44	38,57,16N	107,11,57W	7,156'	Junction: to Marble.
16	10.17	38,57,17N	107,12,45W	6,976'	Confluence: Ruby Anthracite Creek.
17	12.61	38,57,35N	107,15,6W	6,722'	Wilderness sign.
18	13.28	38,57,33N	107,15,46W	6,726'	Finish at Erickson Springs Campground.

Ruby Anthracite to Beaver Ponds

49

Beaver ponds

Distance	4.56 miles out & back to ponds.
Difficulty Rating	Moderate.
Surface	Mostly packed dirt. Some rocky sections.
Gradient	Moderate.
Average Time	3 hours.
Elevations	TH: 8,645; Highest; 8,645; Loss: -505
Maps	Latitude 40 Aspen, Crested Butte, Gunnison; Trails Illustrated 133. Trail 836
Star Rating	☆☆☆☆

Highlights

Hike primarily through aspen forest. Numerous superb views of Marcellina Mountain, the Ruby Range, and East Beckwith Mountain. The fall aspen color is thrilling. The beaver ponds are photographically special.

> **Directions To Trailhead:** From CBVC, drive west on Kebler Pass Road CR 12 for 19.2 miles. Just west of milepost 14 is the Forest Service sign for Ruby Anthracite Trail 836. Park across the road, or take SUV up the road to the right another 0.1 miles to trailhead sign.

Trail Description

The trail descends moderately on packed dirt most of the way. There are intermittent views with many options for photography. The first spectacular view is at mile 0.58 **23**, where Marcellina Mountain, dressed with golden aspens, shows its massive granite walls. Enter a large meadow **22**. After the meadow, the trail rolls up and down before contouring around to the beaver ponds. In summer, this part of the trail is choked with encroaching vegetation. There are more filtered views along the way, but the aspen forest is thick here. When you arrive at the ponds **21**, walk around to the far end to see reflections of the Ruby Range and Marcellina Mountain. Once above the ponds, you have reached mile 2.28 and could consider turning back **20**.

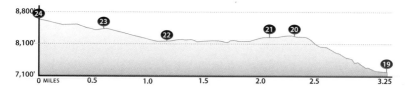

Marcellina Mountain

Meadow views

If you want to go further, it is approximately 1 mile to the bottom of the canyon and Ruby Anthracite Creek. The trail is very steep and slippery, and you will have to come back up 782 feet in elevation when you return. There are filtered views of the canyon and surrounding mountains as you descend, but this part of the trail is also thickly vegetated. The canyon is narrow with steep rock walls.

Views of Ruby Range near start of trail

GPS	Mile	Latitude	Longitude	Elevation	Comment
24	0	38,54,44N	107,13,52W	8,645'	Start Ruby Anthracite to Beaver Ponds.
23	0.58	38,54,43N	107,13,17W	8,415'	Views of Marcellina Mountain.
22	1.16	38,55,2N	107,13,2W	8,179'	Large meadow with grand views.
21	2.06	38,55,37N	107,12,42W	8,194'	Arrive at beaver ponds.
20	2.28	38,55,43N	107,12,50W	8,256'	Beaver ponds turnaround.
19	3.13	38,56,1N	107,12,27W	7,474'	Ruby Anthracite Creek turnaround

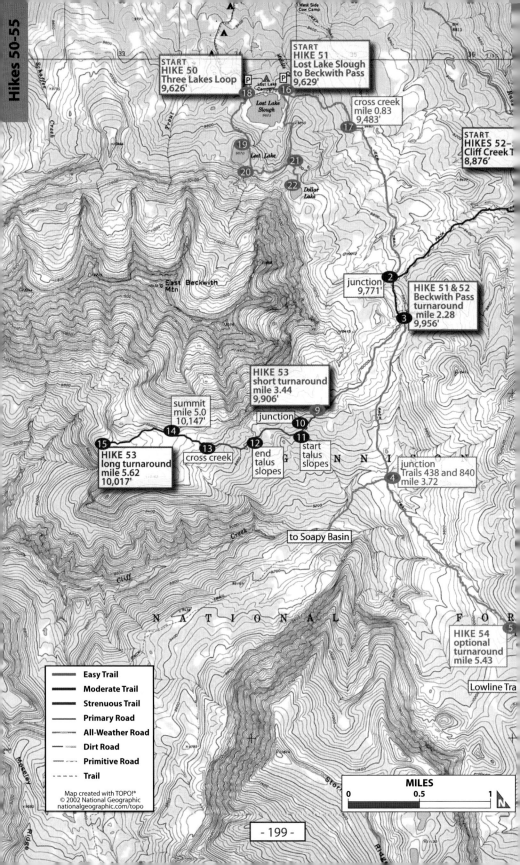

START
HIKE 50
Three Lakes Loop
9,626'

START
HIKE 51
Lost Lake Slough
to Beckwith Pass
9,629'

cross creek
mile 0.83
9,483'

17

START
HIKES 52–
Cliff Creek T
8,876'

18

16

Lost Lake
Slough

19

Lost Lake

21

20

22

Dollar
Lake

East Beckwith
Mtn

junction
9,771'

2

HIKE 51 & 52
Beckwith Pass
turnaround
mile 2.28
9,956'

3

HIKE 53
short turnaround
mile 3.44
9,906'

9

junction

10

11

summit
mile 5.0
10,147'

14

start talus
slopes

15

HIKE 53
long turnaround
mile 5.62
10,017'

13

cross creek

12

end
talus
slopes

junction
Trails 438 and 840
mile 3.72

4

to Soapy Basin

HIKE 54
optional
turnaround
mile 5.43

5

Lowline Tra

Legend

———	**Easy Trail**
━━━	**Moderate Trail**
▬▬▬	**Strenuous Trail**
———	**Primary Road**
―――	**All-Weather Road**
– – –	**Dirt Road**
·–·–·	**Primitive Road**
- - -	**Trail**

Map created with TOPO!®
© 2002 National Geographic
nationalgeographic.com/topo

MILES

0   0.5   1

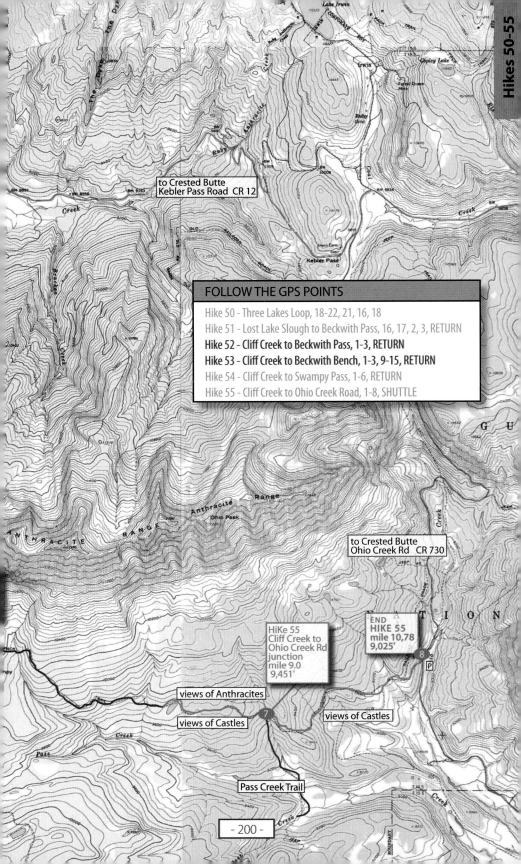

FOLLOW THE GPS POINTS

Hike 50 - Three Lakes Loop, 18-22, 21, 16, 18
Hike 51 - Lost Lake Slough to Beckwith Pass, 16, 17, 2, 3, RETURN
Hike 52 - Cliff Creek to Beckwith Pass, 1-3, RETURN
Hike 53 - Cliff Creek to Beckwith Bench, 1-3, 9-15, RETURN
Hike 54 - Cliff Creek to Swampy Pass, 1-6, RETURN
Hike 55 - Cliff Creek to Ohio Creek Road, 1-8, SHUTTLE

to Crested Butte
Kebler Pass Road CR 12

to Crested Butte
Ohio Creek Rd CR 730

HiKe 55
Cliff Creek to
Ohio Creek Rd
junction
mile 9.0
9,451'

END
HIKE 55
mile 10,78
9,025'

views of Anthracites

views of Castles

views of Castles

Pass Creek Trail

50

Three Lakes Loop

Best viewpoint on trail

Distance	2.81-mile loop.
Difficulty Rating	Easy.
Surface	Rocky much of the way.
Gradient	Easy ascents and descents.
Average Time	1 hour, 45 minutes.
Elevations	TH 9,629; Highest: 9,973; Gain: +506
Maps	Latitude 40 Aspen, Crested Butte, Gunnison; Trails Illustrated 133. Trail 843
Star Rating	

Highlights

Fall aspen color, two spectacular viewpoints of Ruby Range, reflections of East Beckwith Mountain in Dollar Lake.

> **Directions To Trailhead:** From CBVC, drive 16.75 miles west on Kebler Pass Road CR 12. Turn left (S) on CR 706. Drive 2 miles to Lost Lake Campground. Turn left (W) at campground entrance and park near fee sign. Cars can drive to this trailhead.

Trail Description

This is a heavily used trail because it is a short, easy loop that visits three lakes. Lost Lake Slough and Lost Lake are often low on water, so the shorelines may be muddy. Dollar Lake is a beauty set right at the base of East Beckwith Mountain.

Hike this loop counter-clockwise for a gentler ascent. The 0.5-mile ascent to Lost Lake **19** weaves moderately uphill through aspen and spruce forest. There are no views along this section. Past Lost Lake is the grand vista of the Ruby Range and Marcellina Mountain dressed in seasonal golden aspen. (Featured photo)

Then the trail re-enters the trees, climbing gently 0.7 miles to a junction **21**. Take the 0.1-mile side trip to Dollar Lake **22**. At the crest of the hill, there is a lesser path to the left that leads 50 feet to another spectacular viewpoint of the Ruby Range. Descend the short pitch to Dollar Lake, where folks like to fish and just enjoy this beautiful spot. Look for reflections of East Beckwith Mountain and the glittering aspen in the lake.

Back at the junction, the path turns steep and rocky for a while, with limited views. After 0.6 miles, you are working your way around the slough back to the parking area.

View of Lost Lake Slough from trailhead

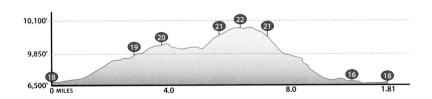

GPS	Mile	Latitude	Longitude	Elevation	Comment
18	0.0	38,52,10N	107,12,32W	9,626'	Start Three Lakes Loop.
19	0.7	38,51,48N	107,12,35W	9,797'	Lost Lake.
20	0.93	38,51,37N	107,12,33W	9,851'	Junction: to falls.
21	1.41	38,51,41N	107,12,10W	9,906'	Junction: to Dollar Lake.
22	1.58	38,51,31N	107,12,6W	9,973'	Dollar Lake.
21	1.81	38,51,41N	107,12,10W	9,906'	Junction: to Dollar Lake.
16	1.51	38,52,11N	107,12,13W	9,629'	Junction: to Beckwith Pass.
18	1.81	38,52,10N	107,12,32W	9,626'	Finish Three Lakes Loop.

Dollar Lake

Lost Lake Slough to Beckwith Pass

Views along trail

Distance	5.3 miles out & back.
Difficulty Rating	Easy to Cliff Creek junction. Moderate to Beckwith Pass.
Surface	Mostly packed dirt. Numerous swampy areas.
Gradient	Mostly very easy ascent. Moderate from junction with Cliff Creek Trail.
Average Time	3 hours.
Elevations	TH: 9,629; Highest; 9,956; Gain:+563
Maps	Latitude 40 Aspen, Crested Butte, Gunnison; Trails Illustrated 133. Trail 842
Star Rating	

Highlights

This is the easiest ascent to Beckwith Pass. There is lovely fall aspen color, and summer wildflowers in season. There are several views of Marcellina Mountain, the Ruby Range, and East Beckwith Mountain on the way to the Cliff Creek junction, though the views are not quite as dramatic as those on the Cliff Creek Trail.

> Directions To Trailhead: From CBVC, drive 16.75 miles west on Kebler Pass Road CR 12. Turn left (S) on CR 706. Drive 2 miles to Lost Lake Campground. Turn left (W) at campground entrance and park near fee sign. Cars can drive to this trailhead.

Trail Description

This route to Beckwith Pass is a much easier grade than the Cliff Creek Trail, but took us exactly the same amount of time because of the added distance. If you are camped at Lost Lake, it is very convenient, but we think the views are much more dramatic along the Cliff Creek Trail.

The trail starts out rocky and remains viewless for the first 1 mile as it winds through spruce forest. After crossing the first stream **17**, the trail gradually opens to seasonal wildflower meadows and aspens. The trail continues with views until shortly before arriving at a junction with Cliff Creek **2**, where you re-enter spruce forest. From this junction, it is 0.32 miles to Beckwith Pass. A short, steep climb of about 0.1 miles emerges from this forest. Now, you can see the summit ahead. This

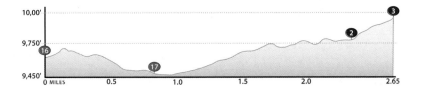

last section of trail is through open meadow overlooking the entire Ruby Range. Awesome!

Once at the summit, you have multiple choices for continuing. See hikes 53-55. Another good option is to return via the Cliff Creek Trail, which is more scenic, but that would require setting up a shuttle (for shuttle directions see directions to trailhead for hike 52).

Views expand as the trail ascends gently.

GPS	Mile	Latitude	Longitude	Elevation	Comment
16	0.0	38,52,11N	107,12,13W	9,629'	Start Lost Lake Slough to Beckwith Pass.
17	0.83	38,51,56N	107,11,33N	9,483'	Cross creek to open meadows.
2	2.33	38,50,50N	107,11,10W	9,771'	Junction: go right (S).
3	2.65	38,50,33N	107,11,6W	9,956'	Beckwith Pass summit. Turnaround.

Ruby Range from Beckwith Pass

Cliff Creek to
52 Beckwith Pass

Distance	4.56 miles out & back.
Difficulty Rating	Moderate.
Surface	Mostly packed dirt with some short, rocky sections.
Gradient	Moderate. Elevation gain is gradual with one short steep section.
Average Time	3 hours.
Elevations	H: 8,876; Highest: 9,956; Gain: +1,075
Maps	Latitude 40 Aspen, Crested Butte, Gunnison; Trails Illustrated 133. Trail 840
Star Rating	☆☆☆☆☆

Highlights

Multiple spectacular views of the entire Ruby Range dominate this hike. It is especially dramatic in the fall, when the Ragged Wilderness peaks are surrounded by golden aspen or capped with a fresh snowfall. This is just a small portion of the largest contiguous aspen forest in the U.S.A. Creative photographic opportunities abound throughout the entire hike. As you hike uphill, the views are often behind you.

> Directions To Trailhead: From CBVC, drive west 12.4 miles on Kebler Pass Road CR 12. Turn left (S) at Forest Service sign for Cliff Creek Trail. Cars can drive to this trailhead.

Trail Description

The trail starts out through healthy aspen forest, soon joined by meadows filled with seasonal wildflowers. The grade alternates between short, steep sections followed by comfortable, resting grades. After you cross Cliff Creek for the first time, spectacular views of the Ruby Range emerge. Keep looking behind you as you climb.

At the junction with Lost Lake Slough Trail **2**, there is an old, steeper route to Beckwith Pass that still looks used. Continue straight ahead to where the Forest Service built a stairway. Ascend steeply out of the creek drainage for about 0.1 miles. Soon you will enter more wildflower meadows and can see the summit ahead. This last section of trail features views of the entire Ruby Range. It is simply breathtaking. Once at the summit, you have multiple choices for continuing. See hikes 53-55. These hikes take you into the lush meadowlands of the West Elk Wilderness.

View of Ruby Range from trailhead

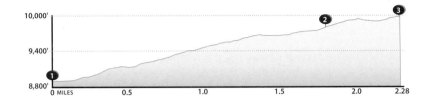

GPS	Mile	Latitude	Longitude	Elevation	Comment
1	0.0	38,51,39N	107,9,50W	8,876'	Start Cliff Creek to Beckwith Pass
2	1.79	38,50,50N	107,11,10W	9,771'	Junction : to Lost Lake Slough.
3	2.28	38,50,33N	107,11,6W	9,956'	Summit Beckwith Pass. Turnaround.

Ruby Range dominates the views on this hike

Cliff Creek to Beckwith Bench

Author at summit of Beckwith Bench

Distance	11.24 miles out & back. (Shorter option: 6.88 out & back.)
Difficulty Rating	Moderate with 1.33 miles of difficult. (Shorter option: easy).
Surface	Easy packed dirt most of the way with 1.33 miles of very rocky walking.
Gradient	Moderate to Beckwith Pass. 1.33 miles of steep descent and ascent to get to bench.
Average Time	7 hours. (Shorter option: 4 hours, 30 minutes.)
Elevations	TH: 8,876; Highest: 10,147; Gain: + 1,678; Loss: -541
Maps	Trails Illustrated 133. Trail 845
Star Rating	

Highlights

Amazing fall aspen color, hillsides covered in summer wildflowers, views of East Beckwith Mountain, Swampy Pass, and southern portion of West Elk Wilderness area. Spectacular views of entire Anthracite Range.

> **Directions To Trailhead:** From CBVC, drive west 12.4 miles on Kebler Pass Road CR 12. Turn left (S) at Forest Service sign for Cliff Creek Trail. Cars can drive to this trailhead.

Trail Description

Read the description for hike 52 to **3**. After reaching the summit, go through the stock gate. There are three unmarked trails. The left trail goes downhill to Swampy Pass **6**, and the hard right trail along the fence goes uphill to high viewpoints near the base of East Beckwith Mountain. Take the middle trail, which stays fairly level, to Beckwith Bench.

For a shorter option **9**, you can hike out about 1 mile on this easy trail. You will know when to turn back, as the trail suddenly dives through an aspen grove into a deep drainage. For the full hike, continue down into that drainage. You experience a very different environment from the expansive views. Look for a narrow, unmarked fork in the trail **10** to the right about fifty feet before arriving at the edge of the beaver ponds. Do not go around the bottom of the beaver ponds as the Trails Illustrated map shows. The correct trail is above the ponds. After the fork, cross the first of four huge talus slopes **11**. Ascend about 400 feet in 1.5 miles through rocky terrain. Suddenly, the aspens give way to a grassy bench. Follow the trail to the highest point, where an island of evergreens stands alone. The featured photo was taken here **14**.

View of the Anthracite Range

Beckwith Bench is to the right in the photo

Start down the gentle slope from the evergreens in a northwesterly direction. The trail completely disappears, but the slopes are wide open and any path you take downhill will get you to the farthest viewpoint. Keep walking about another mile. You will reach the western edge of the bench as it drops precipitously to Cliff Creek **15**. Directly across the chasm are the West Elk mountains. In fall, the golden aspens blanket steep mountainsides. Awesome!

Mike crosses the first talus slope.

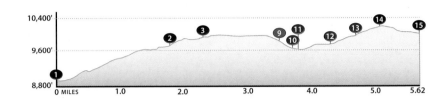

GPS	Mile	Latitude	Longitude	Elevation	Comment
1	0.0	38,51,39N	107,9,50W	8,876'	Start Cliff Creek to Beckwith Bench.
2	1.79	38,50,50N	107,11,10W	9,771'	Junction: to Lost Lake Slough.
3	2.28	38,50,33N	107,11,6W	9,956'	Beckwith Pass summit.
9	3.44	38,49,52N	107,11,52W	9,906'	Short hike turnaround.
10	3.65	38,49,45N	107,12,1W	9,685'	Take lesser trail to right above beaver ponds.
11	3.72	38,49,42N	107,12,5W	9,621'	Start talus slopes..
12	4.22	38,49,39N	107,12,33W	9,754'	End talus slopes.
13	4.63	38,49,37N	107,12,56W	9,975'	Cross creek. Expansive views again.
14	5.0	38,49,43N	107,13,20W	10,147'	Summit Beckwith Bench.
15	5.62	38,49,38N	107,13,57W	10,017'	Turnaround.

View into West Elk Wilderness from turnaround

Cliff Creek to Swampy Pass

View of East Beckwith Mountain

Distance	12.02 out & back. Go as far as you wish.
Difficulty Rating	Moderate to Beckwith Pass. Easy to Swampy Pass.
Surface	Mostly easy packed dirt all the way.
Gradient	Moderate to Beckwith Pass. Very gentle descents and ascents to Swampy Pass.
Average Time	8 hours.
Elevations	TH: 8,876; Highest; 10,407; Gain: +2,049; Loss: -532
Maps	Latitude 40 Aspen, Crested Butte, Gunnison; Trails Illustrated 133. Trails 840, 438, 439
Star Rating	☆☆☆☆☆

Highlights

For hillsides of summer wildflowers or fall aspen color, inspiring views of East Beckwith Mountain, Anthracite Range, Storm Ridge, the West Elk mountains and Wilderness area, this hike is guaranteed to thrill the senses. Dramatic scenery surrounds you from the first step to the last.

> **Directions To Trailhead:** From CBVC, drive west 12.4 miles on Kebler Pass Road CR 12. Turn left (S) at Forest Service sign for Cliff Creek Trail. Cars can drive to this trailhead.

Trail Description

Read hike 52 to **3**. After reaching the summit, go through the stock gate. There are three unmarked trails. The hard right trail along the fence goes uphill to high viewpoints near the base of East Beckwith Mountain. The middle trail goes to Beckwith Bench. The left trail goes downhill to Swampy Pass, your destination.

The trail gently descends about 532 feet for 1.5 miles through clumps of aspen. Gradually, more and more vistas open in every direction. You are entering the wide open meadows of summer wildflowers of the West Elk Wilderness area.

Just after an unnamed creek **4** is the junction to Soapy Basin. Go straight ahead. Start an easy ascent of 646 feet for the next 1.5 miles. The views remain open to within 1 mile of the summit. The views from Swampy Pass **6** are not as thrilling as the hike to it. You may opt to make your turnaround point **5** just before entering the spruce forest and reduce the out & back mileage by 2 miles.

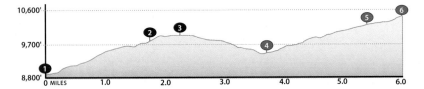

View of Anthracite Range

Aspen clumps

GPS	Mile	Latitude	Longitude	Elevation	Comment
1	0.0	38,51,39N	107,9,50W	8,876'	Start Cliff Creek to Swampy Pass.
2	1.79	38,50,50N	107,11,10W	9,771'	Junction: to Lost Lake Slough.
3	2.28	38,50,33N	107,11,06W	9,956'	Beckwith Pass summit.
4	3.72	38,49,23N	107,11,14W	9,441'	Junction: to Soapy Basin.
5	5.43	38,48,18N	107,10,01W	10,195'	Junction: to Lowline Trail. Optional turnaround.
6	6.01	38,48,10N	107,9,25W	10,407'	Swampy Pass summit. Turnaround.

View of West Elk Wilderness

Cliff Creek to
Ohio Creek Road

View from Swampy Pass

Distance	10.78 miles from trailhead to shuttle point.
Difficulty Rating	Moderate to Beckwith Pass. Easy from Beckwith to Ohio Creek road.
Surface	Mostly easy packed dirt. More rocky on the east side of Swampy Pass.
Gradient	Moderate to Beckwith Pass. Very gentle descents and ascents to Ohio Creek Road.
Average Time	7 hours.
Elevations	TH: 8,876; Highest; 10,407; Gain: + 2,192; Loss: - 2,044
Maps	Latitude 40 Aspen, Crested Butte, Gunnison; Trails Illustrated 133. Trails 840,438,439
Star Rating	

Highlights

Hike primarily through aspen forest. Numerous superb views of Marcellina From Cliff Creek to Swampy Pass is a 6 star hike. The east side of Swampy Pass is mostly through spruce forest with only three views of surrounding peaks. The best part of the east side is the last mile, where views down the Ohio Creek Valley are stunning.

> **Directions To Trailhead:** From CBVC, drive west 12.4 miles on Kebler Pass Road CR 12. Turn left (S) at Forest Service sign for Cliff Creek Trail. Cars can drive to this trailhead.
>
> **Shuttle:** From CBVC, drive west 7.31 miles on Kebler Pass Road CR 12 to Ohio Pass Road CR 730. Turn left (S). Drive car 5.2 miles to signed trailhead. Parking lot & outhouse.

Trail Description

The beginning of this hike, from Cliff Creek to Swampy Pass, is the best of the best. For fall aspen color with expansive views, it is superb. Read the description and see the photos for hikes 52 and 54 to ⑥.

Descending down the east side of Swampy Pass, the trail turns very rocky and enters thick spruce forest. By about mile 8.5, the forest changes to aspen and there are views of the Castle and Anthracite Ranges through the trees. Near the Pass Creek Trail junction ⑦, there is another view of the Castle Range from a small meadow. From here to the end of the trail, it is a very nice walk through sweet smelling aspen that shimmers with golden color in the fall. When you reach a big

View of Castle Range

View of Anthracite Range

meadow and can see the other side of Ohio Pass, look behind you for one last view of the Ohio Creek Valley with the Castle Range in the distance.

Another way to see this part of the trail is to hike from the Ohio Pass Road side. Ascend at least 1 mile beyond the Pass Creek Trail junction **7** to get to the various viewpoints. It is a pleasant walk through beautiful aspen forest. The total out and back is about 5.5 miles.

View of Castle Range

End of trail

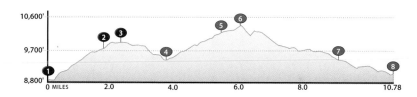

GPS	Mile	Latitude	Longitude	Elevation	Comment
1	0.0	38,51,39N	107,9,50W	8,876'	Start Cliff Creek to Ohio Creek Road.
2	1.79	38,50,50N	107,11,10W	9,771'	Junction: to Lost Lake Slough.
3	2.28	38,50,33N	107,11,06W	9,956'	Beckwith Pass summit.
4	3.72	38,49,23N	107,11,14W	9,441'	Junction: to Soapy Basin.
5	5.43	38,48,18N	107,10,01W	10,195'	Junction: to Lowline Trail.
6	6.01	38,48,10N	107,9,25W	10,407'	Swampy Pass summit.
7	9.0	38,47,39N	107,6,43W	9,451'	Junction: to Pass Creek Trail.
8	10.78	38,48,5N	107,5,14W	9,025'	Finish at Ohio Creek Road.

Ohio Pass Road

Ohio Pass Road (CR 730) turns south off of Kebler Pass Road, about 7 miles from Crested Butte Visitor Center. It provides an alternate, mostly dirt road route to Gunnison that winds down through beautiful ranch country. The backdrop is the Castle peaks. The area is a rolling sea of golden aspen color in the fall.

The road is one lane wide for about 1 mile south of the Ohio Pass summit. There is not enough room for trailers, but cars can drive the entire road. There are several dispersed campsites for small and medium units.

There are 5 hikes (6 if you walk up Swampy Pass from this side). All but Unnamed Lake are through the beautiful aspen forest that characterizes this area. They are short hikes, on relatively easy trails, well suited for families, small children, and adults who are looking for a tranquil, wilderness experience.

View of Castles along Ohio Pass Road

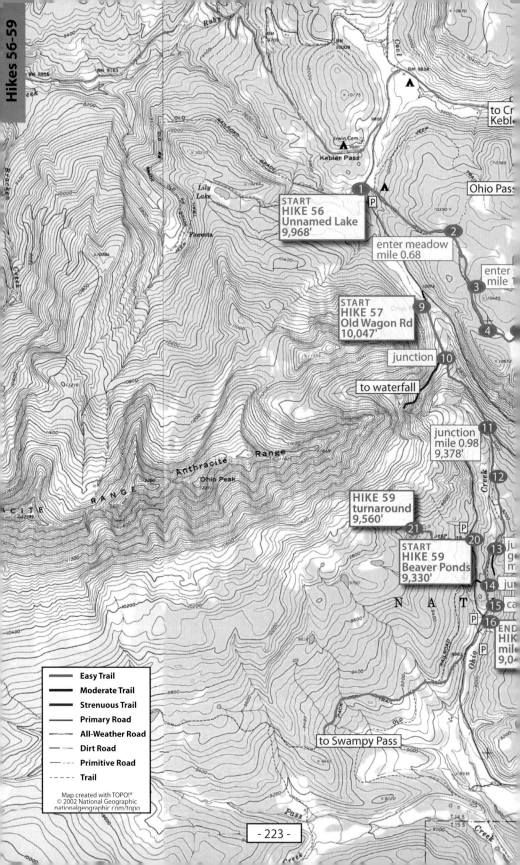

START
HIKE 56
Unnamed Lake
9,968'

enter meadow
mile 0.68

enter
mile

START
HIKE 57
Old Wagon Rd
10,047'

junction

to waterfall

junction
mile 0.98
9,378'

HIKE 59
turnaround
9,560'

START
HIKE 59
Beaver Ponds
9,330'

to Swampy Pass

Ohio Pass

to Cr
Kebl

N   A   T

Anthracite   Range

Ohio Peak

RANGE

to waterfall

Legend

— Easy Trail

— Moderate Trail

— Strenuous Trail

— Primary Road

— All-Weather Road

— Dirt Road

— Primitive Road

--- Trail

Map created with TOPO!®
© 2002 National Geographic
nationalgeographic.com/topo

FOLLOW THE GPS POINTS

Hike 56 - Unnamed Lake, 1-8, SHUTTLE
Hike 57 - Old Wagon Road, 9-16, SHUTTLE
Hike 58 - Old RR Grade, 17-19, RETURN
Hike 59 - Beaver Ponds, 20, 21, RETURN

Splains Gulch Rd
9,560'

8 P

END
HIKE 56
mile 3.5
10,147'

7

enter spruce
mile 2.98
10,220'

Green Lake

Mt. Axtell

Gibson

HIKE 58
turnaround
old culverts
and cairn
mile 1.0

to Green Lake
and Carbon Peak

Grade

18
sign
0.58

19

Carbon Peak

MILES

0   0.5   1

N

Unnamed Lake

Distance	Shuttle 3.50 miles. Out & back 4.06 miles.
Difficulty Rating	Easy.
Surface	Small loose rock on packed dirt; meadows near lake.
Gradient	Easy.
Average Time	2 hours, 30 minutes.
Elevations	TH: 9,968'; Highest; 10,405; Gain: 551;
Maps	Trails Illustrated 133. No trail numbers.
Star Rating	

Highlights

Wildflower meadows surrounding a pristine lake in an area that is visited infrequently.

Unnamed lake

Directions To Trailhead: From CBVC, drive west 7.31 miles on Kebler Pass Road CR 12 to Ohio Pass Road CR 730. Turn left (S). Drive car 0.45 miles to a dispersed campsite. Park.

Shuttle: From CBVC, drive west 5.56 miles on Kebler Pass Road to Splain's Gulch Road. Turn left (S). Drive SUV 1.3 miles. Cross stream to parking area.

Trail Description

This trail can be hiked all the way through with a shuttle, or out & back. The following description begins at the Ohio Pass Road trailhead because the driving access is the easiest.

This trail has no name or number. From the parking area, walk towards the campsites in the trees. An old road leads southeast. The trail climbs comfortably through thick spruce forest for about 0.6 miles. The surface is small loose rock on packed dirt.

The forest opens up and seasonal flower–filled meadows spread out ahead. There are no aspen trees on this entire hike, so plan to enjoy the summer flower season. Look behind you as you advance through this first meadow to view Ruby Peak **2** .

The trail seems almost flat now as it re-enters spruce forest for a short time **3** . Then, when you break out of the forest, you step out into the large, expansive meadowland that surrounds the unnamed lake. Spring through fall, this area is wet **4** . The trail gets lost in this lush meadowland. Leave the trail and walk to the lake **5** .

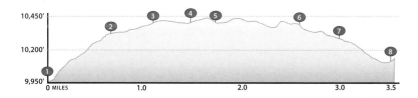

Walk around the lake on the west and north side. Choose your own route, as there are only bits and pieces of trail. Do not cross the outlet stream. Walk a little farther north, away from the lake, to a high point and look out over more beautiful flower meadows. This is a good turnaround point for hikers who did not shuttle **6** .

If you have a vehicle waiting on Splain's Gulch Road, continue on. In spring, stay as high above the meadow bottom as you can. You can see an old road ahead. Walk northwesterly to meet the old road where it first appears out of Splain's Gulch. Once on this road, it's an easy walk down the gulch to your vehicle.

Meadows on route to Splain's Gulch

GPS	Mile	Latitude	Longitude	Elevation	Comment
1	0.0	38,50,46N	107,5,58W	9,968'	Start Unnamed Lake.
2	0.68	38,50,31N	107,5,21W	10,290'	Enter meadows. Views behind.
3	1.10	38,50,12N	107,5,10W	10,343'	Enter spruce again.
4	1.48	38,49,57N	107,5,0W	10,351'	Leave trail. Walk towards lake.
5	1.73	38,49,57N	107,4,48W	10,405'	Lake shore. Go west around lake.
6	2.03	38,49,58N	107,4,34W	10,404'	Good turnaround for out & back.
7	2.98	38,50,13N	107,3,44W	10,220'	Enter spruce to finish.
8	3.50	38,50,32	107,3,43W	10,147'	End hike.

Much of the trail passes through spruce.

Old Wagon Road

Views of Ohio Creek Valley along upper half

Distance	2.31 miles from start to shuttle point.
Difficulty Rating	Easy.
Surface	Upper half is mostly loose rock; lower half is easy packed dirt.
Gradient	Easy downhill.
Average Time	1 hour, 15 minutes.
Elevations	TH: 10,047; Highest: 10,047; Loss: -1,012.
Maps	Latitude 40 Crested Butte, Taylor Park; Trails Illustrated 133. No trail number.
Star Rating	

Highlights

This is an easy trail descending through aspen forest. It follows the historic old wagon road that crossed Ohio Pass. Upper half of trail has good views of the Ohio Creek Valley. Lower half has limited views, but is a very pleasant walk through aspen forest. Not heavily used. Excellent for children.

Directions To Trailhead: From CBVC, drive west 7.31 miles on Kebler Pass Road CR 12 to Ohio Pass Road CR 730. Turn left (S). Drive 1.28 miles to the unmarked pass. Turn right (S). Drive 0.1 miles to a small parking area. There is a trailhead sign.

Shuttle: Back on Ohio Pass Road, drive south another 3.82 miles to an unmarked junction just 100 yards above the Swampy Pass Trailhead parking lot. That unmarked road is where the trail ends. Park there, or at the Swampy Pass Trailhead parking lot. If you only want to walk the upper half of the trail, drive south on Ohio Pass Road approximately 2.17 miles from the pass to a pull off area with a wilderness restriction sign. The trail crosses Ohio Pass Road just 100 feet up from this parking spot.

Trail Description

This trail follows the historic old wagon road that crossed Ohio Pass. The trail starts out rocky, but the gradient is very easy to descend. Spruce and aspen forest are open and allow for views of the surrounding peaks. At mile 0.38, there is a smaller trail heading southwest **10** . That trail goes to a waterfall, a 2 mile out and back trip from the trailhead. The waterfall trail is very overgrown, and parts

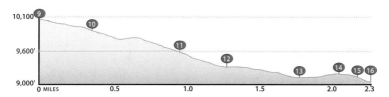

View up valley from lower section

of the rocky talus slopes have washed away, leaving a very narrow path. The end is very steep and slippery.

Continuing on the main trail, enter the healthy aspen forest that makes this valley famous. The trail becomes easier. Views of the Ohio Creek Valley are framed by the golden fall color. It's about a 30 minute walk to Ohio Pass Road **11** . You could park a shuttle vehicle here for a shorter hike.

To continue the rest of the way, cross the road and walk uphill about 50 feet to a very obvious secondary road taking off to your right (S). This road goes all the way to the end of the hike. It is a very peaceful walk through aspen forest.

There is a beautiful, dispersed campsite at mile 1.31 **12** . When you reach a junction of roads, go right, up the hill **13** . The left trail goes to private property. Just ahead, there is one more junction and another dispersed campsite **15** . The short road uphill to the right goes quickly to Ohio Pass Road. Go straight ahead. In another 0.2 miles, the trail will run into Ohio Pass Road again. Your shuttle vehicle should be parked here, or just down the road at the Swampy Pass Trailhead parking lot.

Beautiful aspen forest

The lower trail passes through aspen

GPS	Mile	Latitude	Longitude	Elevation	Comment
9	0.0	38,50,5N	107,5,30W	10,047'	Start Old Wagon Road.
10	0.38	38,49,47N	107,5,23W	9,893'	Trail to waterfall.
11	0.98	38,49,23N	107,5,2W	9,378'	Ohio Pass Road. Walk uphill 50 feet.
12	1.31	38,49,6N	107,5,0W	9,256'	Nice campsite. Easy SUV access.
13	1.81	38,48,41N	107,5,1W	9,072'	Road Junction: go right uphill.
14	2.09	38,48,28N	107,5,4W	9,220'	Junction: go straight ahead.
15	2.21	38,48,21N	107,5,2W	9,147'	Dispersed camp on hillside. Views.
16	2.31	38,48,17N	107,5,4W	9,045'	Finish at Ohio Pass Road.

Old Railroad Grade

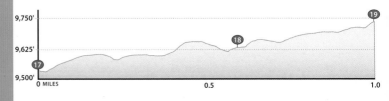

Distance	2.0 miles out & back.
Difficulty Rating	Easy.
Surface	Very difficult railroad rock.
Gradient	Very easy.
Average Time	1 hour.
Elevations	TH: 9,416; Highest; 9,589; Gain:+201
Maps	Latitude 40 Aspen, Crested Butte, Gunnison; Trails Illustrated 133. Trail 436
Star Rating	

GPS	Mile	Latitude	Longitude	Elevation	Comment
17	0.0	38,49,15N	107,4,34W	9,416'	Start Old Railroad Grade.
18	0.58	38,49,9N	107,4,1W	9,589'	Single track trail begins.
19	1.0	38,49,5N	107,3,34W	9,575'	Rock cairn. Faint trail to right. Turnaround.

Highlights

Historic old railroad grade with spectacular views of the Ohio Creek Valley and Castle Rocks. It's a short hike with instant views and awesome photographic opportunities.

towards Ohio Pass

Directions To Trailhead: From CBVC, drive west 7.31 miles on Kebler Pass Road CR 12 to Ohio Pass Road CR 730. Turn left (S). Drive car 2.8 miles to unsigned left hand turn that is difficult to make with a big vehicle. Drive 0.15 miles to a limited parking area by the historical sign.

Trail Description

This is the original railroad grade for the Denver & South Park Railroad through Ohio Pass from Gunnison. Construction began in 1881, but was abandoned in 1882 before any tracks were laid. Standing at the sign, you can look up to see the great rock wall constructed to create a railroad bed for the train. The walk, of course, is barely uphill because RR grades are generally mild, but the footing can be very awkward because much of the trail was built using very large rock as a base material. It is like walking across a major talus slope.

In a very short time, you will see astounding views of the Castle Rocks surrounded by aspens. Camera shots look west, so the best time for photos is morning to early afternoon.

By mile 0.58 **18**, the wide railroad grade turns into a single track trail marked by a sign for Carbon Peak. Continue up this easy trail, through aspen forest, about another 0.42 miles. Keep your eyes open for a large cairn **19** on the right in a grassy, open area. A faint trail leads down into the gully. This is where the railroad constructed a switchback to reach Ohio Pass. The old rock culverts serve to pass water under the raised switchback.

This is the turnaround point for this hike. The Carbon Peak Trail continues up valley at a very easy gradient for approximately 2 more miles before it splits and climbs to Green Lake, or Carbon Peak. It passes through open aspen and spruce forests.

You traverse very rough rock for much of the trail.

Beaver Ponds

Ponds reflect Anthracite Range

Distance	1.0 mile out & back.
Difficulty Rating	Easy.
Surface	Easy packed dirt.
Gradient	Moderate.
Average Time	1 hour.
Elevations	9,330; Highest; 9,560; Gain: +252
Maps	Latitude 40 Crested Butte, Taylor Park. Trail 516

Star Rating

GPS	Mile	Latitude	Longitude	Elevation	Comment
20	0.0	38,48,44N	107,5,12W	9,330'	Start Beaver Ponds.
21	0.49	38,48,47N	107,5,34W	9,560'	Beaver ponds.

Highlights

Walk through a beautiful mature aspen forest with a healthy under-story of ferns and wildflowers. Beaver ponds reflect a portion of the Anthracite Range.

> **Directions To Trailhead:** From CBVC,drive west 7.31 miles on Kebler Pass Road CR 12 to Ohio Pass Road CR 730. Turn left (S). Drive 4.12 miles to signed turnoff to Beaver Ponds, where there is ample parking.

Trail Description

This is a popular easy walk entirely through aspen forest with a pretty under-story of ferns and flowers. It is a good trail for children. The trail is packed dirt and ascends at a moderate grade. There are no views along the trail.

You can walk all the way around the ponds on a variety of paths that might get lost in the wildflowers on the west side. The best photos are of reflections from the southwest end of the ponds facing northeast (featured photo). There are nice sites for setting a tablecloth on the ground or taking a snooze. There are also good tent sites but no facilities.

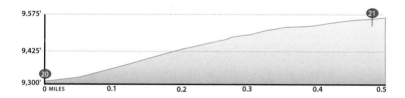

Trail ends at ponds

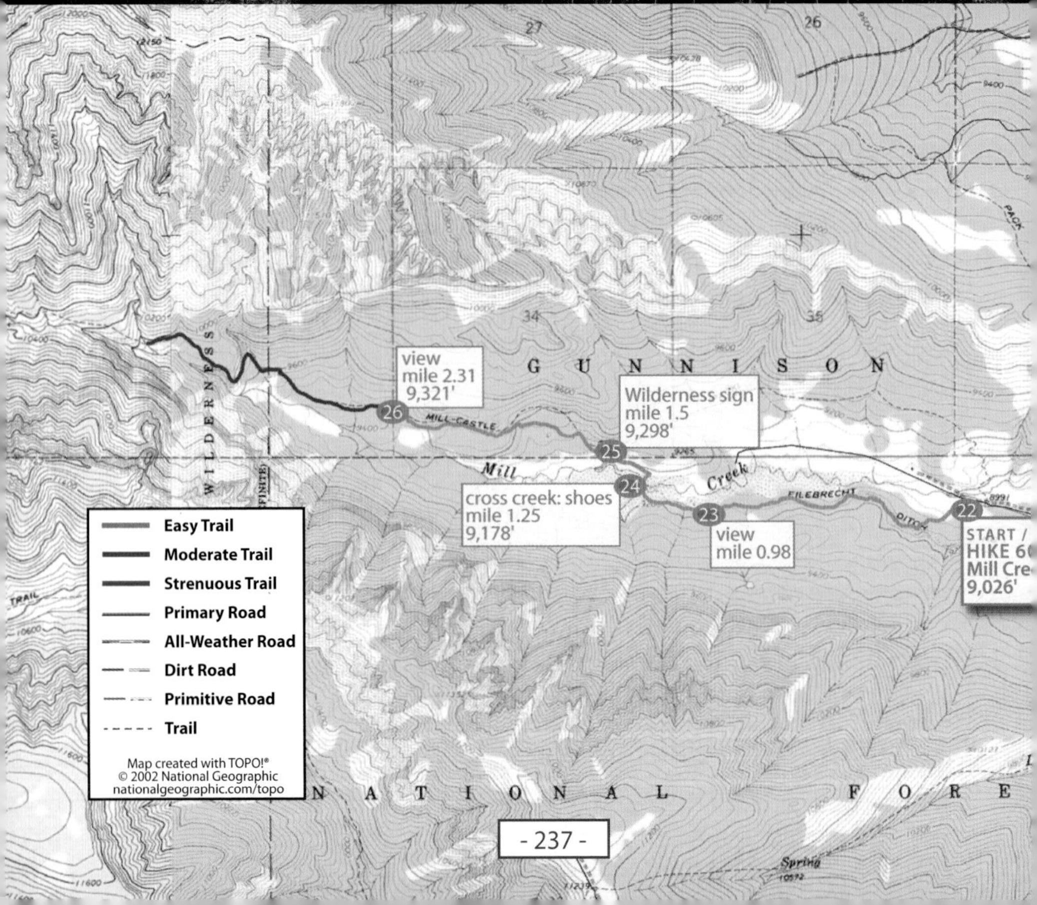

Easy Trail
Moderate Trail
Strenuous Trail
Primary Road
All-Weather Road
Dirt Road
Primitive Road
Trail

view
mile 2.31
9,321'

Wilderness sign
mile 1.5
9,298'

cross creek: shoes
mile 1.25
9,178'

view
mile 0.98

START /
HIKE 60
Mill Cre
9,026'

G U N N I S O N

MILL-CASTLE

Mill

Creek

FILEBRECHT

DITCH

WILDERNESS

N A T I O N A L   F O R E

Map created with TOPO!®
© 2002 National Geographic
nationalgeographic.com/topo

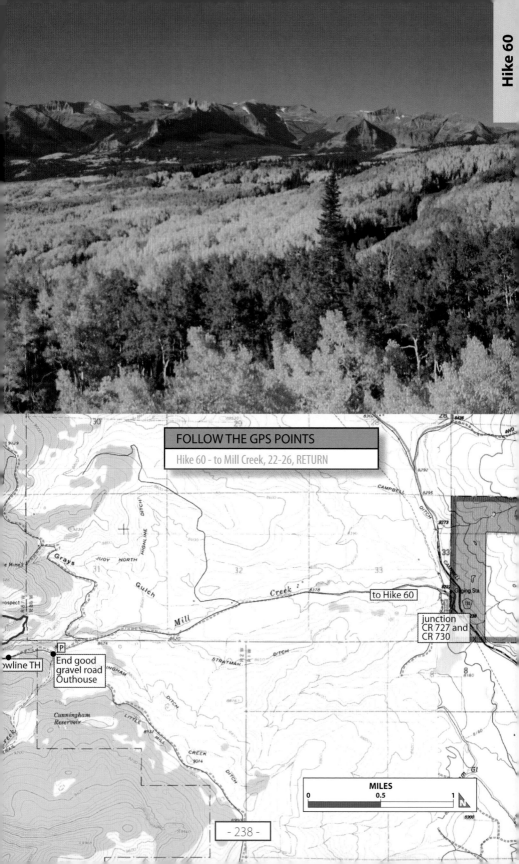

FOLLOW THE GPS POINTS

Hike 60 - to Mill Creek, 22-26, RETURN

to Hike 60

junction
CR 727 and
CR 730

End good
gravel road
Outhouse

owline TH

MILES

0   0.5   1

Mill Creek

Meadow view

Distance	2.5 miles out & back to creek crossing, or hike any distance beyond.
Difficulty Rating	Easy.
Surface	Easy packed dirt.
Gradient	Very easy to creek.
Average Time	1 hour, 15 minutes to creek.
Elevations	TH: 9,026; Highest: 9,178 Gain: +175
Maps	Latitude 40 Aspen, Crested Butte, Gunnison. Trail 450
Star Rating	☆☆☆☆

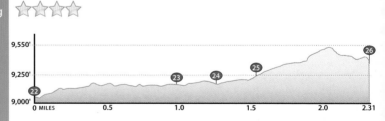

GPS	Mile	Latitude	Longitude	Elevation	Comment
22	0.0	38,41,40N	107,4,25W	9,026'	Start Mill Creek.
23	0.98	38,41,40N	107,5,24W	9,029'	Viewpoint.
24	1.25	38,41,45N	107,5,40W	9,178'	Cross creek. Best views here. Optional turnaround.
25	1.50	38,41,50N	107,5,49W	9,298'	Wilderness boundary.
26	2.31	38,41,58N	107,6,38W	9,321'	View of pinnacle.

Highlights

A great walk with children, this wide, very easy trail travels along side the same type of pinnacle rocks that make up the Castles. Views as far as the Wilderness boundary.

Directions To Trailhead: From CBVC, drive west 7.31 miles on Kebler Pass Road CR 12 to Ohio Pass Road CR 730. Turn left (S). Drive 14.3 miles to CR 727. Turn right (W). Drive 3 miles to a parking lot with an outhouse. The road becomes narrow and rocky, but cars can drive all the way (1.4 more miles) to the trailhead. Past a large meadow, the road deteriorates. Park here, and walk another 100 feet to the signed trailhead.

Trail Description

The trail starts out moderately uphill through aspen and spruce, but there are numerous, tantalizing views of the rock formations through the forest. Soon, it is almost a flat walk on a wide, old road.

By mile 0.98 **23** , an opening shows off the rock walls to the north. Then, quickly, the big meadow affords views up valley and of the southern rock walls as well. This is the best view area of the hike **24** .

If you cross the creek, you may need wet shoes until mid-September. It is a short climb up a hill to the Wilderness boundary **25** for more views of the pinnacles.

If you go beyond the Wilderness sign, the trail becomes a little steeper, and enters a mix of aspen and spruce forest. There are very few views of the wonderful rocks from this point on until you go about 3.5 miles out. Some of the forest is mature and very beautiful, but there are also many sections of deadfall that are not as attractive. If you go 2.31 miles, there is another small meadow with a view of the pinnacles **26** . The trail gains 489 feet in elevation to that point. If you go beyond this meadow, you re-enter forest until mile 3.5. That section gains an additional 560 feet in elevation.

Rock walls to the north

Campsite Descriptions

ID	Mile	#	Size Units	Facilties	Elevation	Comments
Gothic Valley & Paradise Basin Dispersed Campsites						
A	9.83	4	Small	Outhouse	9,614'	Gothic FS Fee Camp in spruce forest.
B	9.84	8	6 small, 2 large	None	9,611'	Washington Gulch TH in Spruce & meadow. Long RVs can park in meadow.
C	10.21	5	5 medium	None	9,699'	Hilltop. In Spruce & meadow. Long RVs can park in meadow, but access road is rough and narrow.
D	10.41	4	3 large	None	9,681'	Must cross East River. Very rocky road. No big RVs.
E	10.83	1	Small	None	9,771'	Parking area for horse trailers. Big RVs camp here when no other space available. Leave room for horse trailers. Last big turnaround on Gothic Road. Big RVs should not go further.
F	10.84	1	Large	None	9,782'	Walk-in tent site. One small parking spot.
G	11.09	6	Tents	None	9,841'	Walk-in tent sites in meadow. Parking for 3 vehicles stacked behind each other.
H	11.44	3	Tents	None	9,996'	Really bad access road. Last site down steep hill requires 4x4 to exit during heavy rain.
I	11.59	1	Small	None	10,072'	Nice site overlooking river. Easy access.
J	12.25	1	Medium	None	10,366'	Overlooks Gothic Valley. Easy access.
K	14.08	5	Small	None	10,417'	West Maroon TH. Sites in trees, or park in meadow.
L	13.87	1	Medium	None	10,692'	Paradise Basin Road. In spruce trees.
M	14.07	1	Medium	None	10,555'	Paradise Basin Road. In spruce trees.
N	14.09	1	Medium	None	10,572'	Paradise Basin Road. In spruce trees.
O	15.66	3	Medium	None	11,317	Various sites around Lake at Yule Pass summit.

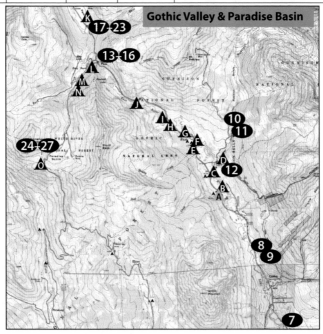

Gothic Valley & Paradise Basin

ID	Mile	#	Size Units	Facilties	Elevation	Comments
Washington Gulch Dispersed Campsites						
A	5.75	4	Small	None	9,645'	Several tents.
B	5.90	6	Large	None	9,656'	Large meadow. Several large RVs.
C	5.75	10	Large	None	9,649'	Large meadow. Many large RVs.
D	5.85	5	Medium	None	9,657'	Rough access road to many camper sites.
E	6.18	1	Medium	None	9,648'	Flat site close to road.
F	6.65	1	Small	None	9,939'	Tent site in trees.
G	6.75	1	Small	None	9,911'	Tent site in trees.
H	7.08	1	Small	None	9,980'	Truck camper or tent in trees.
I	7.81	1	Small	None	10,094'	Truck camper or tent in trees.
J	9.51	5	Medium	None	10,994'	Large sites in open, but large RVs cannot negotiate the narrow road to the pass.

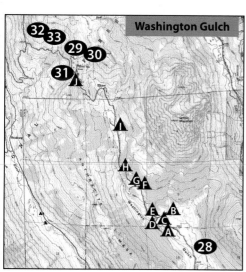

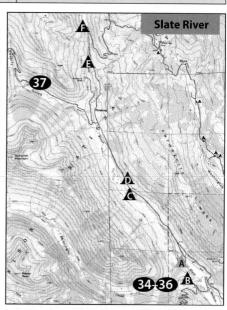

ID	Mile	#	Size Units	Facilties	Elevation	Comments
Slate River Dispersed Campsites						
A	4.6	30	Medium	Outhouses	8,941'	Slate River Forest Service. Many diverse sites.
B	4.6	3	Small	Outhouses	9,002'	On rough road past Slate River campground.
C	5.8	10	Large	None	9,108'	Large meadow for big RVs. Trees for tents. On river.
D	5.97	3	Large	None	9,120'	Overlooks river. Open meadow.
E	8.29	1	Small	None	9,520'	Truck camper or tent. Overlooks river.
F	8.95	6	Large	None	9,467'	Side road to large meadow. Many spots. Near river. Last place to turn around before one lane road.

ID	Mile	#	Size Units	Facilties	Elevation	Comments
Kebler Pass Dispersed Campsites						
A	6.63	5	Large	None	9,771'	Large meadow across from Lake Irwin Road.
B	7.25	1	Small	None	9,892'	Lake Irwin Road. Right on dirt track.
C	7.77	4	Small	None	9,985'	Lake Irwin Road. Forest Service sites. In Spruce.
D	9.51	25	Medium	Outhouse	10,323'	Lake Irwin Campground on lake. Fee site.
E	9.70	2	Medium	None	10,350'	On rough road past Lake Irwin Campground. Views.
F	7.58	2	Small	None	10,023'	Kebler Pass Forest Service site in spruce.
G	8.06	3	Medium	None	9,917'	Side road. Last 2 sites quiet. Views.
H	10.12	1	Small	None	9,212'	Narrow, rocky road. In spruce.
I	10.88	1	Medium	None	8,966'	Near road. Level. Easy access. In spruce.
J	11.68	1	Medium	None	8,872'	In open. Above creek. Easy access.
K	12.17	30	Large	Outhouse	8,862'	Horse Ranch Park. 7 day limit.
L	12.33	2	Large	None	8,838	Cliff Creek Trailhead. 7 day limit. ·
M	12.77	1	Medium	None	8,802'	Short road into aspen.
N	13.78	5	Medium	None	8,774'	Long road into multiple sites in aspen.
O	15.05	3	Small	None	8,944'	3 roads. Each has one site in aspen.
P	16.63	4	Large	None	8,780'	Large meadow across from Lost Lake Road.
Q	19.2	4	Medium	None	8,589'	In aspen. Across from Ruby trailhead.
R	19.2	4	Medium	None	8,612'	Open meadow at trailhead. Rough access.
S	17.63	8	Small	None	9,100'	Multiple sites along road to Lost Lake.
T	18.63	12	Medium	Outhouse	9,623'	Lost Lake Campground. Fee site. On lake.

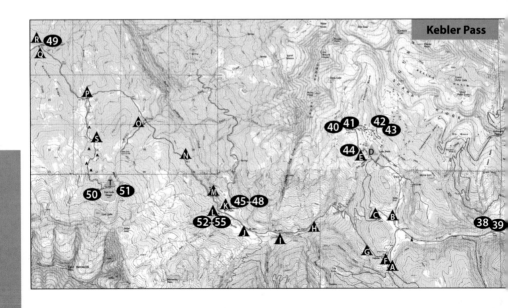

ID	Mile	#	Size Units	Facilties	Elevation	Comments
Ohio Pass Dispersed Campsites						
A	7.72	6	Large	None	9,951'	Trees & meadow sites at trailhead to unnamed lake. Large and medium vehicles should not go beyond here. No turnaround. Access any sites from Gunnison.
B	8.61	2	Small	None	10,121'	Tent sites at Ohio Pass.
C	10.15	1	Small	None	9,506'	RR Grade trailhead. In Spruce.
D	11.06	1	Small	None	9,207'	On lower section of Old Wagon Road. On stream.
E	11.79	1	Medium	None	9,121'	On lower section of Old Wagon Road.
F	12.12	2	Medium	None	9,104'	Junction: Ohio Pass Road & Old Wagon Road.

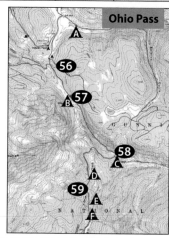

Summer Events in Crested Butte

Crested Butte Visitor Center
601 Elk Ave. Po Box 1288
Crested Butte, Colorado 81224
1-800-545-4505

June 19-21	Wildflower Rush Mountain Bike Race
June 24-28	Fat Tire Bike Week
About July 4	Wildflower Festival Crestedbuttewildflowerfestival.com
July 4-31	Music Festival Crestedbuttemusicfestival.com
August 2-3	Festival of the Arts Crestedbutteartfestival.com
August 11	Annual Crested Butte Summit Hike for Cancer Benefit
August 14-17	Wild Mushrooms Festival

These dates change from year to year and are only approximate. Check with the Visitor's Bureau for updated information.

Meet the Authors

1970, when Anne and Mike married, they formed a relationship based on the mutual need to explore the world by boat, by bicycle, and by foot. A first canoe trip expanded into fourteen years of wilderness canoe explorations and class IV whitewater kayaking adventures. It was during this time that Anne, wanting to record their adventures, started writing, photographing, and publishing stories in various outdoor magazines.

For winter entertainment, they telemark skied in British Columbia's backcountry. For many years they trekked into the various huts and skied the glaciers and surrounding mountains of this winter wonderland.

In 1984, they took up bicycle touring. They bicycled from Costa Rica to Peru. In successive years, they bicycled from Alaska to Idaho; six months through New Zealand; six months around Australia; and finally, a six month journey from Bali, Indonesia to Hong Kong, China.

From 1984 to 1990, they instructed downhill skiing in Vail, Colorado. During the summer months, they instructed Outward Bound Courses in the Boundary Waters Wilderness area of northern Minnesota.

By 1990, backpacking Canada's wilderness trails became the new focus. For six summers, they returned to explore new areas, photograph, and write.

In 2004, they started hiking Colorado's more than 4,000 miles of trails. When they went to Crested Butte, they knew they had found a hiker's paradise. For four summers, they researched, hiked, photographed and mapped this marvelous area, and produced this guide.

Visit their website, www.hikingbikingadventures.com to see all their adventures in photos, books and magazine articles. An E-book download version of this guidebook is available on this site.

Anne is an Alpha and has dedicated this book to the Alpha community. Alpha-1 is a lung emphysema that is inherited. It is progressive and life-long. She had lost 30% of her lung capacity before the disorder was discovered and abated through augmentation therapy. There are only 10,000 Americans currently diagnosed correctly, with a potential 100,000 possible cases. An estimated 20 million Americans are carriers of the abnormal genes. At risk groups include chronic COPD, irreversible asthma, and emphysema sufferers. Her goal is to bring awareness of the disorder to a public place. For more information, go to www.alpha-1foundation.org or call 1-800-5621-3025